Praise for
Meet 100 People

"Meeting new people is vital for everyone in this new economy. Don't be afraid. Pat Hedley makes effective networking accessible to everyone. She keeps it real and she's in your

—Lorraine Ash, *Journalist and author*
Meaningful Life

"This book will change your life. *Mee*
view of what is possible, provide the to
and life-supporting network, and understand where you will thrive professionally. I'm so glad Pat Hedley did the hard work to develop such a thoughtful and pragmatic approach. Now go meet 100 people!"

—Lisa Carnoy, *Division Executive, U.S. Trust, Bank of America NYC Market President*

"*Meet 100 People* offers the motivation and inspiration to take your networking to the next level, so you can make valuable connections and build real relationships, rather than just exchange business cards. This book arms you with skills that will serve you repeatedly in your career and life."

—Stephanie Kaplan Lewis, *Co-founder, CEO, and Editor-in-Chief, Her Campus Media*

"The old adage, 'it's not what you know, it's who you know' has never been truer, and Pat Hedley provides a practical guide for making the connections that will enrich your life. Put yourself in position for success—this book will show you how."

—Doug Anderson, *Founder, GEN Z Connect*

"*Meet 100 People* teaches you critical information missing from the classroom and is a must-read for any student. Interesting anecdotes elaborate on specific networking and career-building strategies. Together with the message of polite persistence, Pat Hedley's book provides a roadmap for achieving long-term success."

—Adrian Kingshott, *Adjunct Professor at Fordham's Gabelli School of Business and former Managing Director of Goldman Sachs*

Meet 100 People

Meet 100 People

A How-To Guide to the Career and Life Edge Everyone's Missing

Pat Hedley

The Path Ahead
Greenwich, CT

The Path Ahead, LLC
Greenwich, CT

Printed and manufactured in the United States of America.

ISBN: 978-0-9986515-0-7
PCN: 2017901428

Edited by Laura Himel, Thinkwell Editing
Book design by Laura Himel, Thinkwell Editing
Illustrations by Julie Vaughn, Grey Street Graphics

First Edition

This book was inspired by Lisa
and her advice to my son.

With gratitude to Cathy, for
introducing me to Lisa.

To my family, you mean the world to me.

Contents

Introduction

There are 728 hours in a month, 168 hours in a week, and 24 hours in a day. I challenge you to dedicate three hours this week (just 3% of your waking hours) to reading this book. You will learn lifelong skills that will increase your confidence, expand your job prospects, and enrich your knowledge. In the time it takes to watch one long movie, you can learn how to meet 100 people and build a network that can benefit you throughout your career and your life.

Meeting new people seems like it should be as effortless as breathing. But even with something as simple and automatic as breathing, method matters. When running a race, rhythmic breathing improves athletic performance. When meditating, slow and mindful breathing reduces tension and relaxes muscles. When angry, deep breaths calm you down. Similarly, certain approaches to meeting people can boost the value of those interactions. From years of personal experience, thousands of meetings, and observing dozens of "master networkers," I understand the art of meeting people. I know it is a learned skill, not an innate ability. Unfortunately, there are few classes that teach you how to build a powerful network of valuable relationships.

Over the years, hundreds of people have come to me seeking career guidance. Many were thoughtful, prepared, and proficient in the art of meeting people. Others were less experienced, learning through trial and error, just as I had decades earlier. I know the feeling of "putting yourself out there" and the nervousness associated with meeting new people.

Networking is not a skill that came naturally to me, nor did I come from a privileged background that gave me easy access to connections. My parents were poor immigrants who fled war-torn Hungary with nothing but a desire to improve their lives. In the U.S., my father worked construction during the day, and at night he studied to become a social worker. My mother taught herself English and used her typing skills to start a business from our small apartment.

Since my parents started from the bottom, they welcomed new opportunities because they had nothing to lose. They were forced to meet people in order to find work and build a life. They encouraged me to be fearless and do the same. Because my parents had no connections, I had to establish them for myself. After receiving my MBA from Harvard, I joined a private equity firm where I was the only woman in an industry that is still male-dominated to this day. It was there that I began to understand that meeting people was essential to my career and advancement.

Over the course of my thirty-year career as an investor, I've met with thousands of people from all over the world. They've connected me to experts, directed me to indispensable resources, helped me discover new investments, and in many instances, they became trusted friends and colleagues. Without question, meeting people has been the foundation of my career and the core driver of my success.

In many cases, meeting others resulted in immediate benefits. Occasionally, it led to no direct outcome other than an enjoyable conversation. Sometimes unexpected opportunities arose from meetings that happened many years before. Often these networking conversations led not only to career connections, but to meaningful personal relationships with long-term mutual benefits that went beyond business.

You too can become a "master networker." This book is your coach. It's a how-to guide if you're just starting your career, already in a job, or looking for a new job. *Meet 100 People* is also meant for anyone relocating, re-entering the workforce, or changing jobs. In fact, it's helpful to those undergoing transitions of any kind. *Meet 100 People* is intended to encourage all of us, at any age and any stage, to engage others and build real connections, proactively and purposefully.

In just ten chapters, you will learn how to build a strong network you will cherish all your life. You'll hear the stories of those who have taken on the challenge of meeting 100 people, and step-by-step, you will learn how to build and nourish your network one person at a time.[1]

My advice is simple and validated with tangible results. Meeting 100 people will increase your success and happiness, challenge you to venture outside your comfort zone, and help you reach your goals. You'll start or re-start the process of building your personal brand: who you are and what you can offer. The process of meeting 100 people will increase your self-awareness and social savvy. By adopting a growth-oriented attitude, you will become more resourceful and resilient. Once you've met 100 people, you will feel the strength and value of your relationships. You'll see the benefits almost immediately. Turn the page, and start right now.

---

1. Names of individuals and certain situations have been disguised to protect privacy.

Part 1

Reflect

Chapter One

Meet 100 People to Get Lucky

Network intensely. Luck plays a big role in life, and there is no better way to increase your luck than by knowing as many people as possible.

Byron Wien, Investor and Vice Chairman, Blackstone Advisory Partners

You have it all figured out. You knew what you wanted to be since you were a kid. You did all the right things to pursue your dream. In college, you studied hard, got great internships, received several job offers, and started your desired job right after graduation. Your whole career is planned, and you're off to the races.

This book is for the rest of us. And even if you think you're perfectly poised for success, you too will benefit.

For the nearly three million students who receive associate's and bachelor's degrees annually, today's job market is particularly saturated and presents many challenges, from landing that first job to eventually finding subsequent opportunities to advance.[2] But the difficulties start well before college ends. First jobs are hard to come by. Fewer than 20% of college graduates have a job lined up upon graduation.[3] First-job tenure is shorter

---

2. National Center for Education Statistics, 2013-14.

3. Svrluga, Susan, "More Than 4 out of 5 Students Graduate Without a Job. How Could Colleges Change That?" *The Washington Post*, January 30, 2015.

than ever, and most leave their first job within the first year.[4] Even if you have a job now, you'll likely be looking for another soon. Today's young workers are expected to hold between twelve and fifteen jobs in their lifetime.[5] And it's highly likely that at some point in your career you'll join nearly half the workforce that's self-employed.[6] Get used to job changes and marketing yourself, because that's what the future holds. So how can you get an advantage in this complex, competitive, and ever-changing world?

Believe it or not, you don't need to be an expert in your field right away. But you do need to be an expert in one thing: meeting people. The good news is that networking skillfully is completely achievable with the right tools. Because so few of your peers have this networking know-how, they will lag behind. But you can and will succeed.

Not as Simple as it Sounds

Meeting people on a regular basis may seem easy, but it's not. Many people are discouraged due to fear of rejection, lack of preparedness, or general discomfort. Others recognize that networking is important, but they don't make it a priority. They put off meeting new people with weak excuses such as "I have no time" or "I don't see the value right now" until there's a trigger, such as a job transition or relocation. A strong network is one of the best-kept secrets of successful people, hidden in plain sight. Most people know there is gold to be found in a large network, but few are willing to prospect for that treasure until they really need it. And when the time comes, they don't even know where to start.

---

4. Express Employment Professionals, 2014.

5. Forrester Research, 2016.

6. Freelancers Union, 2014 study indicates that in 2020 over 40% of U.S. employees will be self-employed.

Taylor, College Senior

In my experience, most people find applying for their first job stressful and challenging. Although people realize the job market has become incredibly competitive, few understand how to best navigate the job process. In the beginning, I applied to several companies but struggled to stand out from the crowd. Applying online was like sending my resume into a black vortex where it vanished with thousands of other applications. As I grew more concerned, I reached out to family and friends for help. I was introduced to a business executive, Carla, who gave me the best advice I have ever received. My sole ambition was to get hired, but Carla suggested I focus on a different, simpler goal which would generate the same result with added benefits. She told me, "Meet 100 people."

Taylor, a family friend, is a young man I have known all his life. He is earnest and smart, but felt overwhelmed when he started his job search. He felt like the deck was stacked against him: others had better connections, higher grades, and a head start. He felt pressure from his peers, his family, and most of all, himself. He knew networking was important, but he didn't know how to start. Taylor's story helped me realize that most young people, and even older ones, don't have the basic tools to build networks. Yet those tools are accessible and available to you. Let me share what I have learned.

Benefits of Networking

Direct Access to Jobs

The shortest path to jobs and opportunities is through a well-developed network that will be available when you need it most.

Understanding Trends

The most relevant and current information is in other people's minds. If you want to be well-informed, talk to as many people as possible.

Interviewing with Confidence

Mastering the skillful interchange of questions and answers is invaluable in recruiting, both now and in the future.

Gaining Self-Awareness

During the networking process, you'll learn what you like and don't like from interacting with others. You'll have a better sense of how you can contribute and add value to any undertaking.

Becoming a Connector

When you have a strong network, people will want to know you and will seek your advice. You'll be seen as a valuable resource who can make introductions and open doors for others.

Establishing Benchmarks

Recognizing competence and success is a tremendously useful life skill. Only through meeting many people will you know what "good" looks like.

Finding Mentors

The only way to find out who inspires you the most is by meeting many people. You will learn who you want on your team. The people you spend the most time with have the greatest influence on you. Choose wisely.

Networking is Necessary to Succeed

Very few successful businesspeople, politicians, or leaders will be candid enough to say, "I am really good at meeting people and leveraging my very large network." They'll downplay whom they know and the human resources they have amassed to get ahead. Some guard their networks jealously, not wanting others to be aware of the power they possess. They worry that by revealing the deep network they frequently tap into, others will think they have unfair advantages. They recognize they have a goldmine.

From politicians to CEOs, from top musicians to well-known artists, all high achievers have vast networks, which are the wellsprings of their success. Anyone who has to market or sell a business, product, service, or creative work needs a network to thrive. The advantages that come with strong networks are well-deserved, because these relationships are hard-earned, carefully built, and thoughtfully nurtured over many years.

Find the people whom you admire and can help you be a better person, and keep them close.

I greatly admire Mark Zuckerberg for his habit of setting personal growth objectives each year. Mark wrote on Facebook in 2015, "Every year, I take on a personal challenge to learn new things and grow outside my work at Facebook. My challenges in recent years have been to read two books every month, learn Mandarin, and meet a new person every day."

Even Mark Zuckerberg, the king of social networks, still sees the value of meeting a new person every day. He wasn't just adding a new Facebook friend. He was meeting others face-to-face. That year, Mark purposefully and consistently met 365 new people, and probably many more. You should do this too, whether you're in desperate need of a job or already successful.

You may think that networking is only important for businesspeople, but meeting a variety of people is an art form which photographers, musicians, and artists of every kind need to succeed. I've followed Brandon Stanton's blog, *Humans of New York* (HONY), since its early days, and I had the pleasure of meeting him. Brandon told his story of losing his job as a financial analyst in Chicago, packing his bags, and relocating to New York City with no money or connections. But his love of photography compelled him to set a goal of taking 10,000 photographs of strangers on the streets of New York. He created a blog sharing the photos and the stories of the people he encountered. In 2016, HONY had nearly 20 million followers from the U.S. and abroad. Brandon has written two best-selling books and accepts numerous speaking engagements. Think about how many new people Brandon had to meet to accomplish this.

Byron Wien is a famous U.S. investor, honored several times as a strategist and thinker. Now in his eighties, he continues to work as an advisor to Blackstone Advisory Partners, a major global financial services firm. At his age, he's had ample experience with what works and what doesn't. Byron specifically pinpoints "networking intensely" as a key to his success. In Byron's oft-cited Blackstone Market Commentary, in which he shares lessons learned in his first eighty years, four of Byron's twenty life lessons are related to networking and interacting with others.[7] He recognizes that luck plays an important role in everyone's life, and the way to increase your luck is to actively seek broad exposure to others, which opens up more oppor-

7. https://www.blackstone.com/media/press-releases/article/blackstone's-byron-wien-discusses-lessons-learned-in-his-first-80-years

tunities available to you. He speaks about giving others the benefit of the doubt and assuming that each person you meet "is a winner and will become a positive force in your life."[8] He encourages traveling and suggests getting to know people by asking them about the formative experiences in their lives. By interacting with others in such a way, you are creating a connection to others that will be mutually beneficial.

8. Ibid.

Who You Know and Who Knows You

The best way to learn is through "OPE": other people's experience.[9] Exposure to other people's lives opens a world of new thoughts, contacts, and opportunities. Other people help you learn what you don't know, and even more importantly, they open your eyes to **the things you don't even know you don't know.**[10] Only your willingness to learn and your motivation to meet people will take you into this unchartered territory. It's you who must make the outreach.

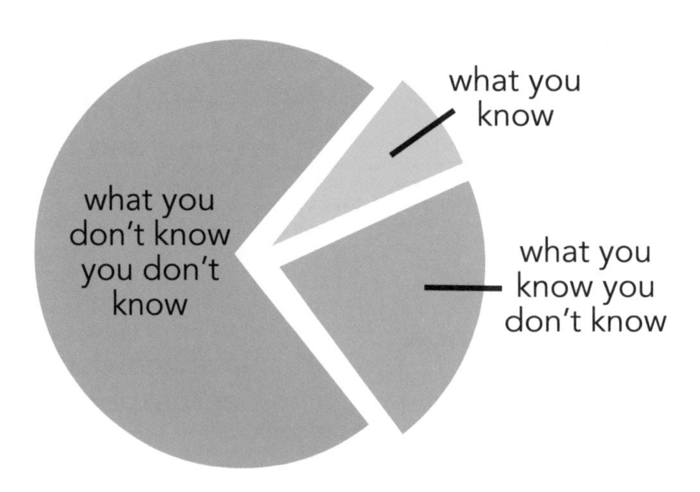

9. Keith Kragh, Chairman and CEO of DocuSign speaking at EY's 2016 Strategic Growth Forum.

10. I learned this useful construct from Beth Chase, founder and CEO of C3 Consulting.

100 People to Establish Your Base Network

Why meet 100 people? Is there something special about that number? Yes, 100 is a hefty even number, a worthy objective which will certainly yield results. It is a great start to a basic network of contacts that will help you grow and learn.

Taylor, Continued

When you first start meeting people for informational get-togethers, it feels like a test. You sit down in front of a person who has achieved the success you want for yourself, and you think, 'If I can just say something brilliant, they'll be so impressed they'll hire me on the spot.' But this is not the point of an informational meeting. After my tenth meeting, it became apparent that the point was not to impress, but to make people aware of you, so that when job opportunities arise, they will remember you. This is what it means to build your network. Sooner or later, wherever you wish to work will be hiring. You want people to remember you when they hear about that opening. The more people you meet, the more people will think of you when an opportunity arises.

I recently heard Simon Sinek, author and optimist, talk about the difference between intensity and consistency. Despite the value our culture often places on concentrated spurts of productivity, intense effort can ultimately only get you so far. He uses the following example to demonstrate his point. If you went to the gym for nine hours for only one day, you would not get in shape. However, if you went to the gym for twenty minutes three or four times per week over many weeks, you would improve your fitness.

The challenge to meet 100 people is a call for consistency, not intensity. It is impossible to meet 100 people in one day. You can't cram networking. You have to build your network brick-by-brick. Meeting 100 people is necessary to establish a regular routine of reaching out and practicing this art on a consistent basis. By meeting 100 people, you will develop a discipline, a habit with long-term payoffs just like exercising regularly. Put yourself among a diverse group of others, and find ways to be near people with whom you can connect and from whom you can learn.

Meeting 100 people is a goal you can accomplish, and one which is guaranteed to improve your skills and your ability to reach specific goals. Even with a conservative estimate of a 1% success rate, you will land that job or win that client.

Nevertheless, you have to manage your expectations for the process of meeting a large number of people. They won't all become close friends or valuable contacts. But my experience is that at least 10% of your meetings can be nurtured into life-long relationships with the right attention and focus, and this will have a huge impact on your career. In every meeting, you're planting a seed for a meaningful connection. Some will take root with time and care. Many will not, and that is okay, too. If you've learned something from a meeting, even if it's how to deal with an uncomfortable interaction or how to improve at asking questions, it was worthwhile.

Once you have hit the 100-person milestone, meeting people will become a regular habit. Your confidence and skills will improve, and your desire to continue meeting people will grow as you see the benefits. The objective is to have a clearly-defined process in order to achieve your goal.

Taylor, Continued

100 people is a magic number. It presents an audacious goal, and is not something you can accomplish in a week or even a month. You have to work at it, and the process of working at it changes you—it makes you more confident and presentable. I am not an extrovert, and it took me a while to find my rhythm and to not get nervous at each meeting. But once I got going, it got easier. While you're working to meet 100 people, you lose your pre-interview nervousness and fear, and you find a desire to keep doing whatever it takes to succeed. In the end, you stop focusing on the number 100. I ended up meeting **108** people before the job offer I really wanted finally came through. I felt like I had done the impossible, and I started my first job two weeks after college graduation.

Networking Isn't Just for Extroverts

Some people are naturally gregarious. They're the life of the party and other people are drawn to them. For extroverts, meeting 100 people may not be so difficult. However, being friendly and outgoing isn't enough to network successfully and maintain close contact with key people over time. You need a plan of action: whom you want to meet, what you want to talk about, and how you can build the relationship so that it is mutually valuable on an ongoing basis.

You may say, “I don’t know many people,” or, “I have a hard time reaching out.” You might point to those who have many contacts and say, “Well, some people are just lucky.” To these naysayers, my response is, “You have to own your fate.” **Make yourself lucky**. As David Schwartz, author of *The Magic of Thinking Big*, says, "**Action cures fear.**" Only you can make it happen.

But What if I'm an Introvert?

Don’t worry! You can learn to network well, too. In her book *Quiet: The Power of Introverts in a World that Can’t Stop Talking*, Susan Cain writes that about one-third of people are introverts, people who have an intrinsic need for solitude and time to reflect and recharge. If that’s you, you can pace yourself and meet people at a rate that is comfortable for you. My curiosity motivates me to meet new people, and I experience real excitement as I learn new things. However, after a very busy day of meeting many people, my energy runs out. I know I need to withdraw, regroup, and re-charge. This self-awareness allows my interactions to be effective and productive.

✧–Rachel, MBA Student

I really dreaded company information sessions when I was looking for a job. The room was full of people all angling to talk to recruiters and hiring managers. Some people felt really comfortable joking and laughing, but I wasn’t one of them. I was much better in one-on-one conversations, so I tended to find someone off to the side, and then I engaged in a more meaningful dialogue. I found that by asking managers what they liked most about their jobs and their company usually initiated an interesting and memorable discussion. This more personal approach worked well for me as I am not naturally outgoing.

Set Your Pace

While the 100-people mark is a lofty goal, you can set achievable objectives to reach it. For Taylor, the process took six months while he was still in college. Work on meeting one new person every day, or two to three people every week. When you're looking for a job, the rate might be even faster. Set your pace at something that feels right for you. But if you only meet one person per month, it will take you nearly 10 years to meet 100 people.

TIME TO MEET 100 PEOPLE

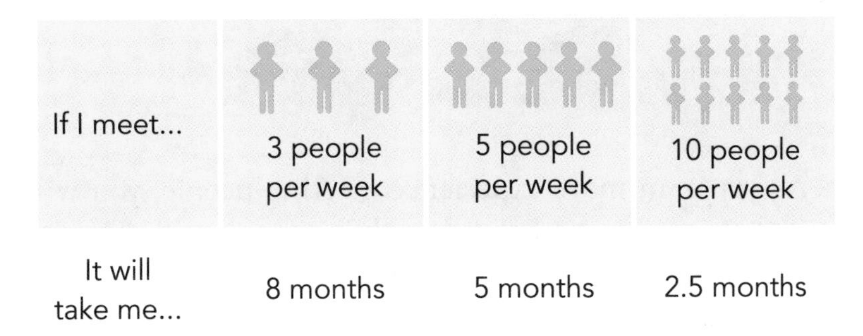

If I meet...	3 people per week	5 people per week	10 people per week
It will take me...	8 months	5 months	2.5 months

A Two-Way Connection

There has to be a two-way connection for you to begin building a valuable network. Every time you meet someone, you're bringing something to the table whether you realize it or not. Regardless of what stage you are in your career, people will respect you for what you can offer, how you conduct yourself, and who you know. Your experiences are unique and only yours. You bring your perspective

Be Smart

Meeting with three to four new people per week is a very reasonable target and will get you to 100 people pretty quickly.

on current events, new trends, and the ways in which the world can be better. Others will want to help you if you're honest about what you don't know, especially if you have the desire and willingness to learn. You can't possibly be an expert in everything, and you will find that you do not have to be. All you need is access to the right people. There is truth in the old adage, "It's not what you know, it's who you know."

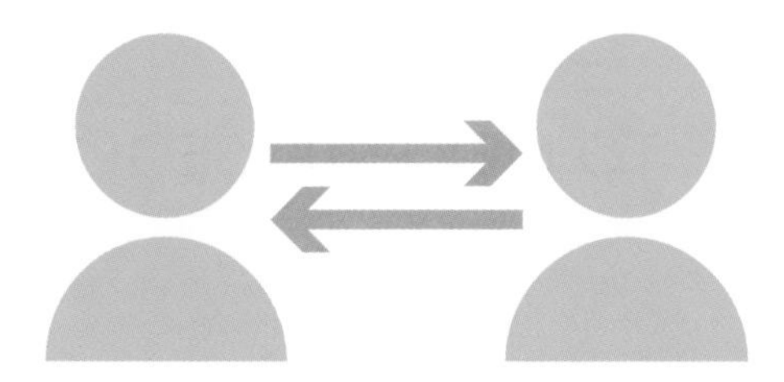

As you gain more experience meeting people, you will learn that you can be helpful to them, too. You'll discover what they need, and your willingness to help will strengthen a productive relationship. A person with a strong network who can access expertise, knowledge, and resources is someone everyone wants to know. You can become this person.

In his terrific book *Give and Take: A Revolutionary Approach to Success*, professor and author Adam Grant describes the nature of most relationships, ones where there's a give and a take. As you seek to meet 100 people, you'll be relying on someone else's willingness to give their time to you. And they will. These individuals will take meetings for many reasons: because others have helped them, because they are doing someone else a favor by meeting you, or because they recognize the value of giving. As Grant so eloquently describes, the real winners are the people who give most freely, and do so because they genuinely want to be helpful. Those who are most generous with their time and resources always benefit in the long run. **This is the true spirit of networking.**

At the beginning, you may be the "taker," but be careful that you don't approach meeting others with a "take-only" attitude. The serial takers give networking a bad name. In time and with practice, you'll find ways to contribute to conversations, share your network, and help others. You will eventually become a "giver." It will be in the "giving" that you will find real connections and really nurture your network.

To get the most out of meeting 100 people, you'll need to identify whom you want to meet, approach them in the right way, and **meet them in person**. It's critical to find a common interest or shared experience and establish a rapport. People are much more likely to help you if they like you.

Think carefully about your interests, goals, and aspirations. You need to know what you'd like to learn and what you'd like to accomplish. Before seeking a connection with someone else, you need to do some important self-reflection. You're the first piece of the connection. Let's find out who you are.

Remember...

∞ **Who you know** and **who knows you** matters as much as what you know.

∞ Intelligent networking results in **ideas, connections, jobs, clients,** and other business and personal relationships.

∞ Networking has to be a **two-way connection** to have the most value.

Chapter Two

⁜

The Process Starts with You

At the center of your being you have the answer, you know who you are and you know what you want.
Lao Tzu, Chinese philosopher

When I encourage people to meet 100 people, the question I'm asked most often, especially by young people, is: "How do I begin?" My answer is **you have to begin with you**. To build an effective network, set achievable goals, and establish a fulfilling career, you must first determine your strengths, weaknesses, values, and ambitions. Who are you, and what do you want?

In many video games and virtual adventures, the first task is to select an identity with the attributes you think will help you win. In real life, we all have identities, too. We define ourselves in many ways: by our family role (son, sister, father), our role at work (financial analyst, doctor, actor), or our interests (athletics, engineering, journalism). The more specific we are in how we define ourselves and what we want to be, the easier it is to find role models who can help us achieve our goals and bring out our best potential.

Defining ourselves and what we want from life requires a certain level of self-awareness which many find difficult to achieve. Psychological profiling guru Tomas Chamorro-Premuzic cites three obstacles to accurate self-awareness:

Be Smart

With self-assessment, the goal is not self-praise or complacency. It is self-improvement.

getting feedback makes us uncomfortable, giving feedback makes others uncomfortable, and negative feedback is unpopular in Western culture.[11] Research by Cornell psychologist David Dunning indicates that people not only overestimate their own abilities, but truly believe their inflated self-appraisals are accurate. Worse yet, since people are generally reluctant to give negative feedback, it's hard to get a clear picture of yourself from others. Be aware of these pitfalls on your path to greater self-knowledge.

Be Honest with Yourself

Doing a self-assessment is easy for some and challenging for others. Some people have a high level of self-awareness and can accurately gauge what they're good at versus what they need to improve. Others have a harder time with self-reflection. Perhaps they've never motivated themselves to go through such a process, or they're afraid to admit their shortcomings.

They're too busy with day-to-day responsibilities to take some quiet time and think about who they are and what they want from their lives. In completing a self-assessment, it's important to be honest with yourself. You may or may not like what you list as your strengths or weaknesses, but it's good to face them, whatever they are. By being honest, you'll realize what you want to build upon, and what you need to improve. Everyone has strengths, just as everyone has ways in which they can grow. **Focus on yours, own them, and be accountable for who you are and what you need to do.** When you discover that

11. Chamorro-Premuzic, "Why You Lack Self-Awareness and What to Do About It," *Fast Company*, March 10, 2015.

you have a lot to improve, view it as a positive outcome and embrace the opportunity.

It's worth getting input from others to ensure that your self-perceptions match up with what others think about you. Talk to trusted confidants. These may be members of your family or your close friends. They could be your teachers, coaches, or counselors. For older or more experienced individuals, it might be your spouse or partner, a therapist, or a work colleague. Know that people don't like sharing negative feedback, so make it easy for them by giving assurances such as, "I need honest feedback to learn and to grow. I appreciate your perspective, and my feelings won't get hurt."

✧-Morgan, College Sophomore

I knew I couldn't meet 100 people without having a clear vision of myself. Taking the time to self-reflect was some of the most productive time I have ever spent. Getting to know myself really paid off. I hadn't given much thought to what my strengths were. The process of taking an inventory helped me realize I have a lot to offer and made me much more confident when talking to people.

The following exercise is a simple inventory of your strengths and weaknesses. The only requirement is to put away any distractions, find a quiet place, and dedicate a certain amount of time to the exercise (thirty minutes is usually a good start). You're investing this time in you. Remember, there are no wrong answers. You can use the blank pages in the back of this book.

Reflection 1: Strengths

Write down five or six things at which you excel. Come up with this list by thinking of things that you enjoy doing and that you've done well. Once you have this list, briefly write down some examples of how you have demonstrated these qualities.

Think about your personality as well. Are you curious, hard-working, focused, energetic, generous or passionate? These are all strengths, which people will respect. Include these personal traits on your list because they make you special. Consider how these strengths relate to a career or job you would like to pursue. You'll be happy when you get to leverage your natural aptitudes to do what you do well.

STRENGTHS[12]	EVIDENCE
Communication	Give presentations often, took public speaking and excelled
Writing	Have a popular blog, do well in writing courses
Analytical skills	Studied engineering, enjoy problem solving
Leadership	Student council officer, captain of the basketball team
Creativity	Known for thinking 'outside the box,' artistic

12. For a long list of strengths, check out the following link: http://examples.yourdictionary.com/examples-of-strengths.html#4lAwSlvdy-ihWlo24.97

Reflection 2: Areas of Development

Now write down five or six things for which you do not have a natural inclination. These may be areas you do not wish to focus on at this time, or conversely, they may be areas in which you would like to learn and improve.

Certain personality traits may be considered weaknesses, such as sensitivity, aggression, or impatience. However, such traits may be helpful in certain professions. For example, sensitivity is essential in being a good healthcare provider, and appropriate aggression and some level of impatience are valuable in sales roles. Weaknesses can be strengths, depending on one's perspective. It's likely you'll be asked about your weaknesses in an interview. Thinking about this in advance allows you to answer in a focused, truthful, and positive way.

WEAKNESSES	EVIDENCE
Communication	Nervous talking to people, stumble over words
Writing	Struggle to produce clear and concise prose
Analytical skills	Difficulty with math and science
Leadership	More comfortable following, dislike the limelight
Creativity	More comfortable with structure and routine

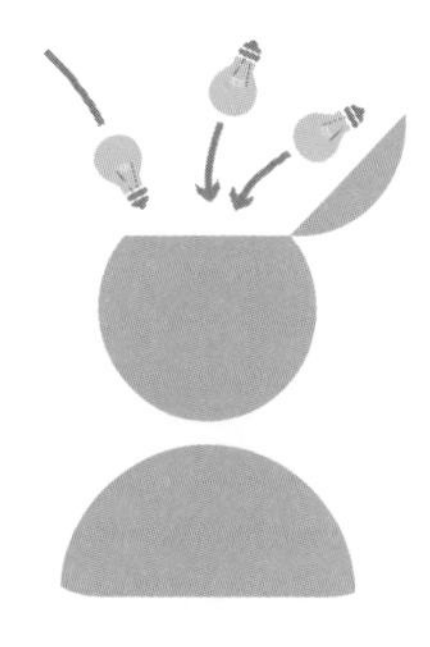

Have A Growth Mindset

So how do you handle your weaknesses? The answer is being open to improvement and adopting a positive attitude. I highly recommend the book *Mindset: The New Psychology of Success* by Carol Dweck, a professor of psychology at Stanford University. Dr. Dweck identifies two types of mindsets: a fixed mindset and a growth mindset. In a fixed mindset, you believe you're born with a certain set of traits and talents, and those qualities are immutable, or fixed. In a growth mindset, nothing is fixed. It is your attitude, hard work, perseverance and your **desire to learn** that allow you to improve in every aspect of your life, including your intelligence. If nothing is really fixed, then **having a weakness isn't permanent**, and it is nothing to be ashamed of. There is a sense of liberation in knowing that you can change, adjust, and grow. Each day is a new day, and you'll keep learning and growing until your last breath. Even Michelangelo, at the age of eighty-seven, is quoted as saying, "I'm still learning."

✧Rakesh, Young Professional

I knew that when I went into some of my interviews, I would be asked things I didn't know. But I also felt it wasn't about getting the right answer. Interviews are really about seeing how you think and react. Whenever I face a situation in which I don't know the answer, I just say, 'I really don't know, but I want to learn,' or, 'I don't know, but this is how I would find out the answer,' or even, 'I haven't thought of that problem before and don't know how to solve it. Would you teach me?' I've found that people react incredibly well when you're honest, show a desire to learn, and ask for help, even in an interview.

In order to deal with your weaknesses in a positive way, you must have a growth mindset. If you want to change and improve, it's within your power to do so. This attitude is an essential aspect of preparing to meet 100 people. People respond well to those who have a growth mindset, because those with a growth mindset are humble, curious, and eager to learn. With a growth mindset, there is no failure. There is only learning. That's what you're doing when you're meeting 100 people: you're learning.

It's really all about attitude, and you'll certainly find this to be true when you start meeting successful people. It's rare indeed to meet a highly successful person who's had no potholes in his or her journey. Many will cite major failures as key turning points in their careers. It was how they faced those challenges that determined their ultimate success.

I'll never forget a story told by a keynote speaker at a major marketing conference. This experienced chief marketing officer was asked to describe her greatest career failure. She spoke about the launch of a baby shampoo in Europe which cost $2 million in marketing spend and was an utter flop. The woman had worked diligently on this launch, and its failure was personally crushing. She went to her boss with her resignation in hand. He said, "I won't accept your resignation. I just made a $2 million investment in your learning, and I won't let someone else benefit from that. Get back to work." The woman redoubled her effort, and after learning from her mistakes, relaunched the product. That time it was wildly successful, and she earned a major promotion.

When talking about failures or weaknesses, the most important thing to consider is what you have learned. If you can describe a silver lining or benefit gained from a bad experience, you'll be ahead of the game. The common traits among those who do well despite setbacks are confidence, a positive attitude, grit, and resilience in the face of adversity. In *Grit: The Power of Passion and Perseverance*, Angela Duckworth, a well-known psychologist, illustrates that true success comes to those who pursue their goals with passion, energy and perseverance. Those who don't give up eventually win. They display "grit," the strength of character that propels them toward their goals. Persistence and perseverance are critical to your meeting 100 people. Successful people got that way by being persistent themselves, and they won't be turned off by your determination. They will respect your grit and want to know you.

Now that you've completed an honest assessment of your strengths and weaknesses, the next step in understanding yourself is reflecting on what you believe in and what you want to achieve.

Values and Goals

Roy Disney of The Walt Disney Company once said, "It's not hard to make decisions once you know what your values are." You wouldn't go on a long road trip without knowing your destination, or having a GPS to direct you. If you don't know where you're going, you'll wander aimlessly. Even if you know where you're headed, you need to know you're traveling in the right direction. Your values are your inner compass.

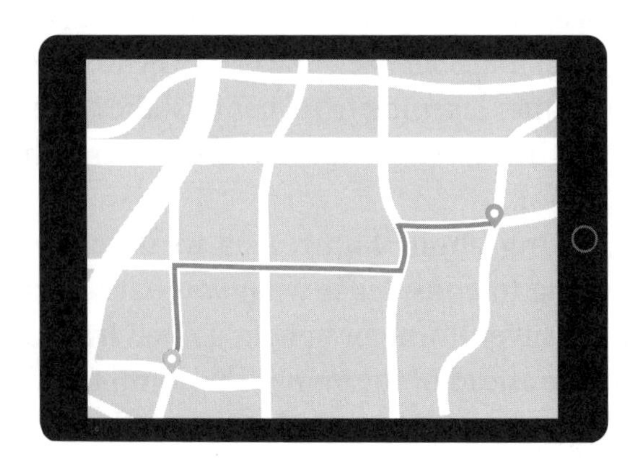

As you journey through life, you should ask yourself: What are my **values**? What are my **goals and objectives**?

→ How am I going to reach my goals?
→ What are the obstacles to accomplishing my goals?
→ How am I going to overcome these obstacles?
→ What sacrifices will I tolerate, and which will I not?

Reflection 3: Values

Many people forget to be in touch with themselves and don't truly understand what they value. Your values are the roadmap for your life. Set aside some time to reflect on your values and write down the five things that matter to you most.

THINGS THAT MATTER[13]	VALUES
Reading and learning	Curiosity
Structured settings	Safety
Parents or children	Family
Helping others	Service, generosity
Delivering on promises	Integrity
Fitness and exercise	Health
Freedom to act alone	Independence
Ability to influence others	Power

13. Longer lists of values can be found at the following web links: https://www.akpsi.org/admin/document.doc?id=486 and https://www.stevepavlina.com/articles/list-of-values.htm

✧-Samantha, College Freshman

In the beginning, I hadn't really thought about what I valued, but it makes sense that what you value helps guide your decisions. You'll make different choices in life if you really think about what's important to you, rather than what you feel like doing in the moment. It's good to challenge yourself on your values because **if your actions don't reflect your values, then something's wrong**. Perhaps you don't really value what you say you value. Perhaps you need to rethink how you approach certain situations. Frankly, I'm so glad I asked myself the question, 'What do I value?' It changed my approach to life.

Reflection 4: Goals

Take some time to outline what you want to achieve in the short term and long term. Knowing your personal and professional goals is important in setting a foundation for how you'll approach people and ask for their help. List five or six short-term goals, things you would like to accomplish in the next two to three years, and some long-term goals, what your view of the "good life" would look like ten to twenty years from now. Most people never take the trouble to sit down, think, and write out what they would like to accomplish or what a "good life" would look like. You'll learn a lot about yourself by reflecting on your goals and writing them down.

There should be a correlation between your values and the goals you've set for yourself. If you know what's important to you, you'll know what conditions you need to create for yourself to excel and be fulfilled. For example, if health is a key value, you should not choose a job or career in which your health will be compromised or endangered through physical or emotional stress. If family is important to you, you won't want to consider a career requiring you to travel or be away from your family for long stretches of time. Every pursuit has some struggle associated with it. It is best to be upfront and aware of the cost as well as the gain. Being true to your values will help you be authentic.

Be Smart

Values count for everything, and should help you create the life you want to lead.

Jerome, College Graduate

I'm not one of those people who's known since they were young what they wanted to be. But I do have an idea of what I'd like to achieve in life. I'd like to travel as part of my work and I like problem-solving. I considered working at a consulting firm, since that would allow me to travel and learn. It was great to get these goals on a piece of paper.

Be Genuine

Before you can go out and meet others, you have to develop both confidence and humility, two traits that may seem in conflict, but are actually complementary. Boastful people are often quite insecure. Confidence and humility engender trust, and people are more likely to help you and want to work with you if they trust you. In *Presence: Bringing Your Boldest Self to Your Biggest Challenges*, Harvard professor Amy Cuddy writes that in social interactions, trust and respect are viewed as even more important than competence. Trust and respect are earned through honesty, consistency, integrity, and concern for others. An alignment of interests is also important. You need to show others that you are not an adversary, but are on their team.

Think about the people you know who embody authenticity and reliability. They are great mentors to have. They will help you gain greater self-awareness. Most people are pretty good at detecting whether someone is genuine or not. When meeting other people, it will become very clear if you're not being candid and sincere. You'll be asked questions such as:

- "Why are you interested in this company or industry?"
- "Who or what inspired you to pursue this career?"
- "Where do you see yourself in five or ten years?"

Smart people will ask you follow-up questions and probe more deeply into your motivations if they notice inconsistencies. These questions will be easy if you are authentic and genuine. They will expose you if you are not. Remember, **there is no wrong answer in being who you are.** Make sure you're honest, answer thoughtfully, and if you don't know something, simply say, "I don't know." People respond positively to people who are well-grounded, consistent, and true. In a recent speech, Jeff Weiner, the CEO of LinkedIn, said, "I am looking forward to the day when being grounded is not a compliment, but an expectation."

Defining Your Goals

Some people are clear in their goals, and they're ahead of the game. If you have a specific goal, such as becoming a doctor, you can identify the steps needed to get there, such as studying the right subjects and getting an internship at a hospital, and anticipate the potential obstacles you'll face, such as long hours of hard work and making contacts in healthcare. Clarity gives you a head start in the process of achieving your goal. The greater the clarity, the clearer the target becomes. If you know what you want, you can articulate it and identify whom to talk to about your specific area of interest.

If you aren't sure, or you're still exploring what you would like to achieve, don't worry. That's why you're casting a wide net and meeting 100 people. Whether or not you know what you want to achieve in life, you'll need to outline what you want from the process of meeting 100 people. A short-term goal may be gathering information and learning, and it might take fifty people to set you in the right direction. A long-term goal may be getting a job in a certain field, industry, or location, so the next fifty meetings will be more targeted. These meetings are meant to help you find your path and start moving.

Talking to many people will help you determine which careers are appealing and which aren't. Remember, you learn as much from deciding what you don't want as you do by discovering what you do.

Sometimes you'll be introduced to someone, and there will be no clear objective. Take a few risks and be open-minded. Accept the meeting. Say yes when someone invites you to an event, a meeting, or a meal. No matter what age you are, there's something to learn. I've gone into many meetings in my life thinking nothing would come out of it. Time and again, I've been proven wrong. There is huge value in meeting people. They can open doors for you that you don't even know exist, or inform you of opportunities you might never have heard about. If you don't know what you would like to do, how do you figure it out? Start with the basics.

6 Steps to Achieve Your Goals

1. List the people you admire and whose jobs sound interesting in your circle of contacts, and reach out to them.

2. Review the courses you've taken. They may give you a sense of what skills you want to utilize, such as writing, problem solving, or communicating.

3. Talk to teachers and counselors who have seen students go on to interesting jobs and can provide introductions as well as insights.

4. Explore the countless career sites, blogs and other resources online where you can learn how to prepare for certain careers and see salary statistics, as well as trends affecting employment.

5. Read books about people who have had the career you wish to pursue. In my teens, I had a real interest in becoming a lawyer, and I devoured any book about, or written by, lawyers. F. Lee Bailey's *The Defense Never Rests* gave me a real view into the legal defense process.

6. Participate in an assessment program which can help determine your strengths and point you in the right direction for potential careers. There are many assessment tools, both online and at career centers. It's well-known that the SAT isn't a predictor of career success. Do well on the SAT if you can, but don't believe that a low SAT score means your career prospects are doomed.

Now that you've reflected on **who you are and what you want,** let's tell your story and **create the mosaic of you.**

Remember...

∞ Set aside time to do an **honest and open-minded self-assessment**.

∞ Adopt a **growth mindset** and recognize that failure is just learning in disguise.

∞ Remember that your **values are a compass for decision-making**.

∞ Ensure that your **values align with your goals and actions**.

∞ Know that people can detect whether or not you are genuine. **Be authentic**.

Chapter Three

⁜

You Are a Mosaic

Telling a story is one of the best ways we have of coming up with new ideas, and also of learning about each other and our world.
Richard Branson, entrepreneur, investor, and philanthropist. Founder of the Virgin Group.

Mosaics are works of art made by arranging small pieces of colored glass, stone, or other materials. Each piece is distinct, and when many are placed together, the resulting work is a beautiful creation showing a rich and colorful whole.

Chapter two encouraged you to get to know yourself. Now, how do you develop your personal story so that when you meet someone new, you're interesting and memorable? How do you take your experiences and express them in a concise and meaningful way which reflects what is special about you? How do you write that perfect resume?

You are a mosaic made up of all your experiences: what you have learned, whom you have met, and where you have traveled. A mosaic is a perfect image to think about as you tell your story. I use this metaphor with students when they apply to colleges, and young professionals as they prepare for interviews. I have them write short anecdotes related to each of their activities and hobbies. The anecdotes tell more than just the bare facts. There must be some related incident that shows their personal traits, such as the effort and perseverance needed to play in the youth symphony, or the courage to overcome fear when traveling on a program abroad.

In creating a "mosaic tile," your goal is to show the learning that resulted from participating in the activity—both the struggle and the success. Those are the stories that resonate and that people remember. They add drama to a conversation and make it more engaging.

✧Leslie, High School Senior

When preparing for college interviews, I knew I'd be asked questions about my activities and schoolwork, but I wasn't sure what to say. Then an advisor suggested writing short stories associated with my activities. I thought of it as my personal iTunes playlist. If I had to talk about my interest in history, I'd tell the story about my trip to Greece. When asked about ice skating, I'd relate the time I broke my arm and the work it took to recover and skate again. I had about eight stories on my 'playlist' and it really worked well.

Building Your Resume

Stories or anecdotes are important as you're building your resume, which is just a written form of the "mosaic" of you. Your resume has three important purposes:

→ To get through the "black vortex" of the **resume scanner**
→ To get past the initial **human screen**
→ To inspire someone to **want to talk to you and meet you**

Once a potential employer has decided to meet you in person, your resume will help them learn about you and connect with you in a meaningful way. A resume will never be a complete picture of you, but it will reflect how you think of yourself and your accomplishments, highlight the skills and abilities you possess, and show the thought and effort you put into creating that mosaic of you.

What you include on your resume will be the template for the conversation you will eventually have with someone. If you already have a collection of mosaic pieces, you'll be able to select those which are most appropriate for your conversation. You won't know what your interviewer will want to discuss, but if it's on your resume, it's fair game. Likewise, it's unlikely you'll be asked about something you haven't included on your resume. Think carefully about the stories you want to tell.

> Be Smart
>
> **When meeting people, you want to share stories that are just like the tiles of a mosaic. Each anecdote should have a clear purpose and reveal something important about your strengths and traits.**

Writing your resume need not be a gargantuan task. Break it down into manageable pieces and focus on one element at a time: your education, your work experience, and your activities. Make sure you have a story related to each section.

Your resume **must:**

→ Be **one page**, easy to read, and not repetitive
→ Highlight your **strengths and achievements**
→ **Quantify** certain skills (such as certifications)
→ Show that you are **hard-working and capable**
→ Give a glimpse into your **interests and hobbies**
→ Leave a memorable, **positive impression**

Resume Real Estate

The resume starts with one 8.5x11" piece of white paper. This is the space you must fill in the most efficient and effective way possible. About 60-70% of the paper's real estate should be dedicated to your work experience, 20-30% to education, and the remaining 10% to other interests and activities. This is for a standard resume. If you're writing your very first resume, you can allocate more space to your education, since that is where you have spent most of your time so far.

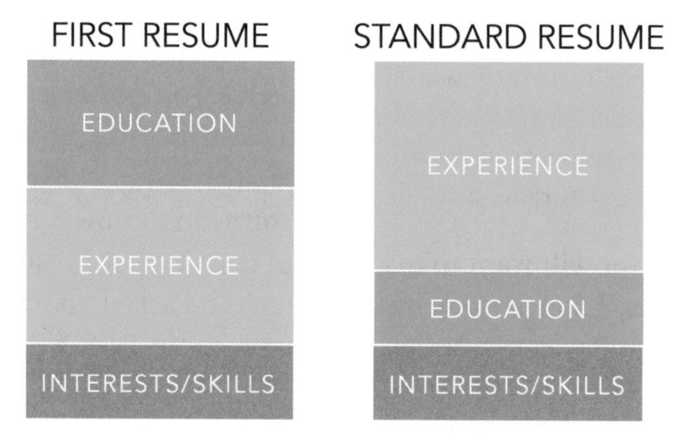

Although the purpose of your resume is to convey information, it also must look clean, neat, and uncluttered. There are many resume formats and resources to help you create one. Don't reinvent the wheel. Use a standard template with the following important elements:

→ **Format**: Clean and easy-to-read, with no typos or mistakes
→ **Layout**: Good use of the paper's "real estate"
→ **Content**: Engaging material for someone to ask questions

The "Parser" and What This Means for You

When applying for a job today, getting past the initial screen involves more than just having human eyes approve your resume. In some instances, you'll be required to submit your resume online, and when you do, your resume will be scanned and "parsed" by a computer. Recruiters use software to extract (or parse) information from resumes and configure it so that it can be easily sorted and searched. This process allows recruiters to manage the hundreds and thousands of resumes submitted online to find the best candidate for a job.

Be Aware

Don't be too creative in formatting, or information from your resume won't be properly parsed.

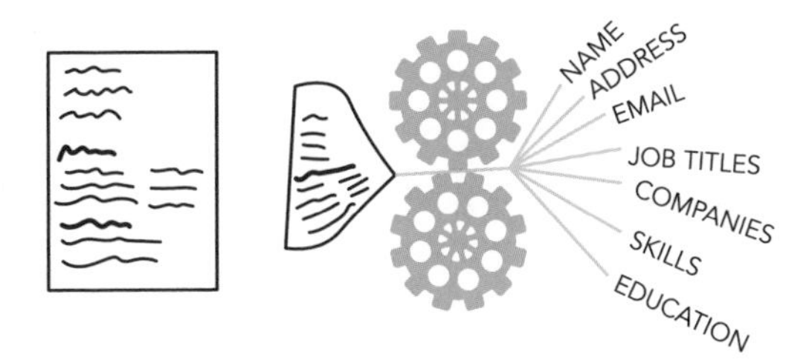

If your resume isn't written in a way which makes this parsing easy, one of two things will happen: either important information will be lost in the extraction process, or your data will be categorized incorrectly and become unsearchable. Therefore, think carefully about using anything other than standard formats and clear language. Straightforward words and headings are better than creative ones. Eliminate unusual fonts, borders, or images. They are irrelevant and will only cause problems. According to the leading parsing company

Sovren, a ".doc" file is the best format to use when submitting a resume online. When sending the resume directly to a hiring manager or a human, I recommend a ".pdf" version.

You're writing your resume both for the parser and for the human reader, who may only see those resumes pre-screened by software. Much of this chapter is oriented towards the human reader, but do not forget to make your resume appropriate for the first step of the screening process. By meeting people in person, you can sometimes sidestep the software screener altogether and get straight to the top of the recruiter's resume pile. It's one of the many advantages of proactively meeting people. Included in the appendix are three sample resumes (see pages 171-173). On the following pages are two standard templates, one for recent graduates with limited work experience, and one for experienced professionals. Model yours in a similar fashion. The templates provide a reliable format with specific guidelines on how information should be presented for both a first-time resume writer and a more experienced professional. Even at Harvard Business School, everyone uses the same standard resume template regardless of the job they are pursuing.[14] The template isn't where you should be creative. If you use a standard template, appropriately-placed information will be readily parsed by the computer, and humans will find relevant information easily as well.

What Employers Want to See

An employer wants to know that you have basic skills and some experience functioning in a work-like environment. This is also relevant for people who have had long job hiatuses. Organizing a 10k run, selling candy for a fundraiser, or serving

14. See additional information: https://www.alumni.hbs.edu/careers/navigating-your-career/making-a-career-change/Pages/resumes-and-cover-letters.aspx

as treasurer of your baseball team all require skills like leadership, organization, and communication, which are valued in the workplace. Athletes are often sought out for jobs because they must possess tremendous discipline, teamwork, and grit to be successful. Volunteering at the hospital, tutoring disadvantaged students, or running the Red Cross Blood Drive shows initiative, caring, and a desire to make a difference. You should certainly include these activities on your resume.

Undoubtedly you'll have faced some adversity in your life. Those situations are tremendous opportunities for personal growth, and they influence who you are today. If you feel comfortable, share what you have learned from your life's challenges. Make sure you include them in your collection of mosaic tiles, because they make you unique.

Be Smart

Remember, your resume isn't a static document. It is never really done. Reviewing, revising, and updating it should be an ongoing habit.

When you're writing your first resume, include summer and part-time jobs, and any other experiences that simulate a "real" job. You might be surprised to learn that even top companies love young people who have worked jobs such as landscaping or flipping burgers. Combined with good grades, manual work experience indicates that you can roll up your sleeves, show up on time, and work hard. Employers want to see people willing to do the grunt work required in almost every entry-level job, and even in many senior roles.

Template for Student or Recent Graduate

J.Q. Example

Address
City, State, Zip

Phone number
jexample@gmail.com

EDUCATION

Name of University Start Date - End Date
Degree title City, State
-Major: Minor:
-GPA: Major GPA:

High School Start Date - End Date
High School Degree City, State
-List relevant coursework
-SAT:

PROFESSIONAL EXPERIENCE

Company Start Date - End Date
Job Title City, State

Use action verbs to discuss what you accomplished in moderately specific terms
-[Bullet 1]
-[Bullet 2]
-[Bullet 3]

SKILLS AND INTERESTS

-Languages
-Skills
-Interests

Template for Experienced Professionals

C.Z. Example

Address
City, State, Zip

Phone number
cexample@gmail.com

PROFESSIONAL EXPERIENCE

Company 1 — Start Date - End Date
Job Title — City, State

Use action verbs to discuss what you accomplished in moderately specific terms

- [Bullet 1]
- [Bullet 2]
- [Bullet 3]

Company 2 — Start Date - End Date
Job Title — City, State

- [Bullet 1]
- [Bullet 2]
- [Bullet 3]

EDUCATION

Name of University — Start Date - End Date
Degree title — City, State

-Major: Minor:
-GPA: Major GPA:

SKILLS AND INTERESTS

-Languages
-Skills
-Interests

As you gain more experience, your accomplishments will grow. Highlight those that have the best stories behind them. Think about the skills you developed, such as attention to detail, collaborating with others, or analyzing information. How you handle tedious work reveals a lot about you. Even boring jobs can have interesting stories and unpredictable positive outcomes.

✧Jasmin, College Senior

My first assignment at my summer internship was to input a list of companies into the firm's database as potential clients. It was a monotonous task, but I'd learned from a previous summer job that when faced with something tedious, it's best to just get it done. So I entered 70 company names and associated information as quickly and accurately as possible. Two hours later, a senior executive came to my desk and asked, 'Are you Jasmin Carter? Did you know that every time a new potential client is entered into the company database, an alert is sent to the full senior leadership team, including the CEO, and he just got 70 emails?' I felt embarrassed until the senior executive continued, 'Keep doing a great job. We love your hard work and strong initiative. Let's just change those alert settings temporarily while you finish your project.' After that I got many more interesting assignments.

This anecdote is a perfect example of a "mosaic" piece Jasmin can retell in interviews. What was most interesting about Jasmin's summer internship was not that she helped create a database of potential clients, but that she could tell a story that showed she was a hard worker with great attention to detail. Of course, Jasmin had no idea that completing her tedious task so quickly would get her noticed at senior levels, albeit in a way that she didn't expect.

Reflection 5: Read Your Resume as If You Were the Employer

Everyone wants to get his or her resume finished, and once it's completed, many people forget the last and most important step: the final review. Set aside five to ten minutes. Print your resume and hold a copy in your hands. Review your resume as if you were doing the hiring. Notice the formatting and make sure the layout is clean. Then look at the words and the messages you're sending. Are you pleased with what you see? If not, no worries—you haven't sent it out yet! Have someone else look over it, too, and make adjustments. Be fully confident that this initial picture of you is what you want potential employers to see.

Top 10 Questions for First-Time Resume Writers

1. GPA: To include or not?

If you don't include your GPA as a recent graduate, the automatic assumption is that your GPA is low. A high GPA is important for some jobs, but not for all. You should know whether your potential employer will place value on your GPA. For many employers, GPA is one indication of how hard you work and how well you have done. If your GPA isn't high, you'll have to explain why. You have to "own it." You cannot be defensive, nor can you ignore it. It may not come up, but it's essential for you to be able to respond properly if it does.

There are many reasons for a low GPA: a high degree of difficulty in course selection, time-consuming extra-curricular activities, personal or family problems, health issues, or perhaps too much socializing. Whatever the case may be, be prepared to explain your situation, and importantly, quickly direct the conversation back to the attributes that make you a wonderful candidate for the job. Countless people with low GPAs have gone on to successful careers. After your first or second job, no one will ask about your GPA.

2. Test scores: To include or not?

The answer is similar to the question above. It depends on the kind of job you're pursuing and whether the test scores matter. If you have a low GPA and high test scores, it's worth including the test scores. If your test scores are relevant to your work, include them. If they are not important for the role you're applying for, only include them if you wish to talk about it.

3. You never graduated: What to do?

You must be clear and accurate when listing your credentials, including where you attended school, for how long, and whether or not your received your diploma. If you didn't graduate, you must indicate that clearly. **You cannot lie on a resume.** If you are not caught immediately, you can still suffer the consequences years later.

The head of college admissions at a prestigious university was fired after a long and illustrious career when it was discovered she misrepresented herself on her resume—she never graduated from college. Not only was she deeply and publicly embarrassed, but her career was ruined. Do not put yourself in that situation.

4. No real job experience: What to do?

If you're applying for your very first paid job and you haven't had an internship or other job in your area of interest, include whatever experiences you've had that show you're a hard worker. I learned from Mark, a senior human resources executive of a Fortune 100 company, that his research showed that the factor most strongly correlated with job success was having had "manual labor" work experience. This includes jobs like painting houses, digging ditches, or busing tables. Include these experiences, as they show that you're willing to roll up your sleeves and get the job done. There is no shame in hard work, regardless of what your career ambitions are.

5. What if I have unusual interests?

If you're willing to talk about it, and it's a genuine interest that reveals something important about your personality, include it. I know a young man who worked in a panda preserve one summer. He loved the experience and had a story to tell, so he included a brief mention of it at the end of his resume. It turned out to be a great conversation starter, and illustrated his willingness to do what was often a dirty, smelly job. You can bet he's asked about that experience every time. He is able to relate the experience to why he is a good hire—he is willing to roll up his sleeves—and that makes both him and his story memorable.

6. Do I include everything I've done?

No, do not include every single extra-curricular activity or job you've ever had. Remember, your conversation will be directed by what's on your resume, and if you include too much, the main message and best stories will get lost in the clutter. You want to paint a clear picture of yourself that is neither overly complex nor confusing. One of the biggest mistakes I encounter on resumes is information overload. I want to see accomplishments rather than job duties. Avoid words like "responsible for" or "duties included," and use action words instead, such as "designed [a new system]," "analyzed and solved [a problem]," "created [a program]," or "resolved [a dispute]." I want to learn whether the individual is self-motivated, ambitious, and hard-working based on what they have done. Quality counts more than quantity. **Less is more**.

7. How do I handle job hops or other gaps?

The best way to handle job hops or gaps is to consider the stories behind them and why they occurred. Job changes are normal in today's economy and can occur for a variety of valid reasons. Generally it is good to stay with an employer for a two-year period of time. That is sufficient time to show some real accomplishments. But sometimes that's not possible, and you have to be prepared to talk about why you made such a quick change. Gaps can occur for many reasons, too. If you have a job gap, it's important to talk about why it occurred and what you accomplished during that period of time.

There are many non-work activities that require work-related skills, such as organization, collaboration, writing, or speaking. These skills are valuable to the right employer, and they can be very useful when meeting people. A gap year after high school and before college might have been one of your most compelling life experiences. Whenever you have a good story to tell, a story which reveals something about your character, your strong personality traits, and why you are a valuable person to have on the team, it's worth including on your resume.

8. Does it make sense to customize my resume depending on the type of job I'm applying for?

If you have multiple interests and are applying for jobs in different industries or functional areas, it can be helpful to customize your resume so that it's most appropriate for the job you're seeking. A resume for your potential acting career is quite different from the resume you would send for a paralegal job you're pursuing until you succeed as an actor.

9. Should I write a cover letter?

Yes. A cover letter allows you to make your case: why you're interested in the job, and what you bring to the table. It should clearly answer the question, "Why should I hire you?" Make it short and to the point. Persuasive cover letters make the reader want to meet you. My friend Harry, who has run several companies and hired hundreds of people in his long career, told me about a cover letter and resume he received from a young salesperson. In his cover letter, the recruit said his strengths were his stamina and perseverance. If given the opportunity, no one would work harder than he would. The enthusiastic letter impressed Harry so much that he immediately called the candidate and asked to meet him. The candidate was as good in person as on paper, and he was hired on the spot.

10. If I lost my job, what do I say?

The fact that you lost your job won't necessarily appear on your resume, but you need to be prepared for what you'll say in the interview. There are many scenarios in which people lose a job for reasons completely out of their control. If this is the case, it is easy to say, "my firm was downsizing," "my department was eliminated," or "my position no longer exists." However, if you got fired for poor performance or something worse, this is more problematic. I am a firm believer in honesty as the best policy. It is better to be upfront and truthful than to be hired for a role and always worry that someone will discover the facts about why you were fired. You'll only lose your job again. If you performed poorly, you must do some self-examination before taking on a similar role. This is why self-awareness and accountability are essential to learning and growing.

You're never really done writing your resume. Regularly weed out what is no longer relevant and add interesting new work and personal experiences. Your resume will change as you grow and develop. Keep it current and make it interesting. Make sure it is clean, correct, and well-formatted. Make your resume a beautiful mosaic of **you**.

Remember...

∞ You are a culmination of all your experiences to date. **Think of your experiences as the mosaic of you**.

∞ Create a **list of anecdotes** you can tell when talking about your experiences. This is your "playlist" of stories about yourself.

∞ **Your resume is a written version of the mosaic of you**. Make sure it stays up-to-date as you grow and your experiences change.

Part 2

Connect

Chapter Four

Find Your Allies

Everyone we meet is put in our path for
a purpose. We are all teachers.
Marla Gibbs, American actress, comedian, singer

In the first part of the book, you became more self-aware, defined your goals, and learned how to present yourself and your experiences in a way that is interesting and memorable. You're ready to meet 100 people. But how do you decide with whom to talk, and how do you reach out to them? How do you increase your chances of someone saying "yes" when you ask to speak with them? **Who are these 100 people?**

You may not realize it, but you already have a network. Everyone has a group of people with whom they have shared experiences, values, and objectives. Our very first network consists of our families and our neighborhoods, people to whom we have close physical proximity. Over time, our networks expand to our classmates, our work colleagues, and other members of organizations we've joined. These are natural networks, people with whom we have "strong ties," which we nourish through regular interactions.[15]

15. Granovetter, Mark, "The Strength of Weak Ties," 1973.

Taylor, Continued

The hardest part of meeting 100 people was figuring out who to meet. I don't think anyone knows 100 people in an industry right off the bat. I asked my professors if they knew anyone who worked at the companies I was interested in, and I reached out to alumni from my college. I asked my parents if they had friends who worked in my industry of interest. And to my surprise, once I had met three or four people, the suggestions kept coming. My list of contacts expanded like a web, and the challenge became keeping track of it all. Organization is paramount. The only way to fail is to reach out to people and not follow up. Then you've wasted the opportunity for additional contacts. You have to be very organized and systematic to be successful. These skills will be valuable to me for the rest of my life.

One Link to Get You Started

All you need is **one person** to get you started on your task of meeting 100 people. The very best thing you can do is **tell people you're looking to meet people.** Get others interested in your goal and have them become your allies. The more people you meet, the more support you'll receive. It is up to you to ask for references and meetings. Do not rely on anyone else to do it for you. You don't have the luxury of being shy or intimidated. **If you don't ask, it won't happen.** Just as soon as you've met one person, you've started the process.

The best starting point to create your list of 100 people is your natural network of "strong ties," as they can lead you to their contacts and expand your existing network. And as Mark Granovetter argued in his landmark paper "The Strength of Weak Ties," it is often new people you are just meeting, the "weak ties," who will become the best sources for job leads and opportunities.[16]

Lessons from Home

My mom became an entrepreneur in the 1960s, building a small business in data processing from our tiny apartment. She came to the U.S. in 1956 with a strong Hungarian accent, little education, and no network. Despite the strikes against her, she forged ahead and started meeting people. Her greatest assets were fearlessness, perseverance, and resilience. She knocked on many doors and faced much rejection, but she never gave up. Her positive attitude helped build her network, and it was her network that opened the doors necessary for her success. A few of these individuals have become lifelong friends, people with whom she is still is in contact fifty years later.

Two important lessons I learned from my mother are to not be afraid of meeting anyone, and to keep going no matter what. Polite persistence is completely underrated, yet it is the real determinant of success in anything you do. You have to have the grit and determination to pursue your goals in the face

16. Granovetter, Mark, "The Strength of Weak Ties," 1973.

of obstacles. I did not start with a strong network either. I was fortunate to receive a great education which helped me build one. But in many ways, I, too, started from scratch. Even now as an experienced executive, I'm still meeting new people all the time: both my peers and people much younger than I am. My network-building is a life-long endeavor, and you should make it one of yours, too.

Some people have a head start in networking because their parents are well-connected or because their college has a strong alumni network. So what? You still can build a great network, regardless of where you start.

Practice Makes Perfect

I recently met a young man named Kenny who is a serial entrepreneur. When building his first business, his goal was to get twenty new clients each week. In his first week, he went out on the streets of New York City and met twenty restaurant owners who were potential customers. He got twenty rejections. He adjusted his pitch and tried again. The second week, he got two people to sign on as clients. Three months into the process, his hit rate was 80%. It was all due to practice and determination.

Another young man named Steve is one of the most impressive young men I have met. Hailing from the Midwest, where he was elected student body president of a 20,000-student university, Steve is earnest, outgoing, and humble. He plans to work in New York City after graduation and constantly meets new people to expand his network. I asked him the secret to his popularity and ability to connect with many people.

✧Steve, Young Professional

How do you go out and meet people? First, make yourself visible. Go places, do things, and be around people you know could help you grow and keep learning. You want to be yourself. If people like you and see you as an authentic person, they'll want to help you. What I've experienced is that people want to help learners, not people who think they know it all. So I always ask a lot of questions, and I am grateful for the time others spend teaching me new things.

Serendipity: At the Crossroads of Openness and Good Timing

Serendipity is one of my favorite words. It holds so much promise, combining the element of surprise with good fortune. The trick with serendipity is that you don't experience it unless you recognize it exists. Serendipity never occurs in complete isolation. You can't get lucky or have good fortune if you're alone at home, far from the action. Good things only come your way if you make yourself visible and initiate the outreach. You have to recognize opportunity and act on it.

Be Smart

There is 100% certainty of what will happen to you if you're alone in your room: nothing. But there is no telling what you will encounter in the process of meeting people.

✧ *Emma, Fiction Writer*

All my life I've wanted to be a writer. After an unexpected relocation that required me to give up my job, I spent two years holed away writing a novel in isolation, making no attempt at friendships or connections in my new town. When the time came for me to publish my book and rejoin normal life, I was paralyzed. Already an anxious introvert, I'd lost all confidence in my ability to interact with others. On the advice of trusted friends, I decided to put myself out there. I attended my first local writer's group literally shaking in my boots, but with each meeting and introduction, I regained my confidence and realized the value of connecting with like-minded others. In less than a year, I knew several literary agents and editors, attended many writing conferences, and became a well-known member of a thriving local writing community. Now I do public book readings and speaking engagements. Making that first venture out the door was one of the most frightening and important steps of my life.

Hot and Cold

The best way to meet someone you don't know is to find someone who knows them and can introduce you. This is called a **warm referral** versus a **cold call,** which is contacting someone whom you don't know at all. **Warm referrals are the best way to reach out to someone**. The person you wish to meet will be willing to talk to you because someone they know asked them to. This isn't guaranteed, but the chances of reaching someone by email, phone, and ultimately in person, are highest with a warm referral. This is how I, and most other very well-networked individuals, meet new people all the time.

How do you get warm referrals? The easiest way is to ask people you already know: your strong ties. These can be your parents, teachers, extended family, coaches, neighbors, and others you know in day-to-day life. These are people with whom you already have a relationship, a good one, and whom you can approach for advice.

✧Erin, College Student

I wanted to get meaningful internships for my summer breaks so that I could get a head start on deciding what to do after graduation. I had taken a few courses in marketing and wanted to learn more. I mentioned my interest to my Aunt Liza, who knew someone in marketing at her company. Aunt Liza called Mia and asked if she would speak to me. Before speaking to Mia, I prepared by writing a list of questions to learn what she did on a daily basis. We had a thirty-minute conversation, and at the end, Mia offered to introduce me to two other people in marketing. Mia even suggested a firm which she knew hired summer interns in marketing, and said she would meet me when I was in New York over break.

Erin started her process by talking to someone she trusted, her Aunt Liza, even though Liza lived 500 miles away. Liza connected her to Mia, someone she knew in marketing, and this warm referral got Erin off to the right start.

You Never Know Who Can Be Helpful

According to "The Strength of Weak Ties" by Mark Granovetter, the real value of a network comes from "weak ties": people who are not necessarily close friends or in your natural network.[17] Granovetter's research shows that of the people who found jobs through personal contacts, the majority found them through weak ties, rather than their close friends. The goal in meeting 100 people is to leverage your strong ties

17. Granovetter, Mark, "The Strength of Weak Ties," 1973.

in order to expand the number of weak ties you can access. Remember, each person is a gateway to many other contacts.

Among the 100 people you meet, there will be those who can directly and indirectly help you. It is best to treat each person as if they can have that direct influence, because you never know who can. Even if your contacts aren't in a position to hire you at the moment, they can expand your thinking about jobs you might like to pursue. Importantly, they can introduce you to others who may be looking for someone with your interests. Most people don't consider that the people you meet today can be excellent contacts in the future. They'll likely get promoted or take on new and better positions, and can be helpful in countless ways down the road. These cultivated contacts are part of your network, and your network will make **you** more valuable over time.

Be Smart

Serendipity rarely finds shy people. Serendipity smiles upon those who are unafraid to take risks and trust others. Break out of your box and put yourself in the path of good fortune.

The way to make life happen for you is to take advantage of every opportunity. You can expand your network in places you might not expect, such as at athletic events, parties, and conferences. Be open to talking to people without a specific goal. You must release any biases you have and interact with a broad group of people, especially those who do not look like you. Make yourself comfortable with people of other generations, ethnicities, races, and genders. You have to be open-minded and free of prejudice to meet 100 people.

Chance encounters can happen anywhere, and you must be ready to utilize them. I recently overheard the following story. Trish, an executive and mother of a college-aged daughter, met a woman named Jan on an airplane. Trish mentioned that her daughter was nervous about her upcoming job search. Jan suggested that Trish's daughter reach out to her. Jan happened to be a career coach who lived near Trish's daughter's college. Trish's daughter reached out to Jan, who helped hone her interviewing skills and write her resume.

A coincidence, maybe, but coincidences don't happen unless you take action and talk to others. You should assume that people are well-intentioned and that they are willing to help. When someone offers something of interest, accept it. You never know.

A young entrepreneur named Nick with whom I work told me he built close to 70% of his network by talking to nearly every seatmate in two years of frequent flying in his early twenties. It was how he was eventually introduced to me. First, Nick met Grant on a flight from Los Angeles to Chicago. Nick emailed Grant afterwards, and they had lunch. Grant introduced Nick to his friend Linda, and Nick had lunch with her several times in Los Angeles. Linda introduced Nick to Bert, and Bert, someone I know and trust, introduced me to Nick. It's a small world, but only if you make it so.

✧Oliver, College Senior

I was excited to go on spring break with my friends. I still hadn't found a summer internship, and a few days skiing in Colorado seemed like the perfect break from the stress. One morning as I was trying to catch up to my friends, I took the singles line and joined three older men. One of them asked me where I was from and what I did. I told him I was a student at Northwestern interested in working in sports marketing. He said, 'I went to Northwestern too.' We bonded over living in Evanston and sailing on Lake Michigan. At the end of the ride, Lucas gave me his card and told me to call him after break. He said he would give me some referrals that might help in my job search. Who would guess that a fifteen-minute lift ride could broaden my network?

Always Give the Green Light

When a person you know suggests you speak to someone, say "yes" right away! You must take people up on their recommendations and offers. Always say yes, even if it is intimidating or difficult. Many people fail on this simple and important task. An excuse I often hear from young people who balk at the idea of asking for a meeting is, "They're probably busy, and I don't want to bother them." **Get rid of such self-defeating thoughts.** You're giving yourself this excuse because you don't want to make the effort. Ask for the referral, ask for the meeting, and ask for the time. Accept every offer for an introduction and reach out to that person.

✧-*Megan, College Student*

I met with Tim, an executive at a bank, based on a referral from my professor. I framed it as an informational interview and knew I wouldn't have much time with him. After a brief introduction, I told him I wanted a summer internship in the real estate department. Tim didn't work in real estate, but to my surprise, he said, 'I was just talking to Mitch in real estate the other day, and they're looking for interns.' He took me over to Mitch right away. It was all very spontaneous and I was really nervous. But I talked to Mitch and ended up with an internship.

Use Online Resources

Technology can be useful, too. LinkedIn's second-degree connection feature is a goldmine. The more people you're linked to, the wider your reach because of their connections. You should have a LinkedIn profile and start adding contacts so you can find even more connections. Facebook is another great tool for finding people who could be helpful to you. Other excellent platforms include GiftedHire, a career preparation site, and school or activity-based online platforms. The goal is to find people who can get you to the people you want to reach.

Be Smart

Older successful people love mentoring and giving back. People enjoy giving advice and being viewed as an expert. You can use this to your advantage. Mention that you are young and seeking advice, and be respectful of your target contact's time and experience.

Making a Cold Call Less Chilly

If you don't have a warm referral for certain people on your target list, think of the following people you can target with a cold call, but with whom you have something in common: a mutually shared background, interest, or activity. Shared experiences provide a connection, and they matter a lot. The following are a few examples of groups of people with whom you may have mutually shared experiences in order to get a warmer reception:

- → **Alumni** from your grade school, high school, or college
- → People from your **town**
- → People who have the **same interests as you**, such as sports or music
- → People **whose work you admire**, whether it be an article or a speech at a conference
- → People in your fraternity, sorority, or any **shared social organization**
- → **Friends of friends**, people in a similar social circle

Generally, cold calls don't have a high hit rate. In sales, you'll likely have to make ten calls or emails for one potential customer, a 10% hit rate. In seeking advice, your hit rate is likely to be much higher. Don't get discouraged. Meeting 100 people will take a lot of work. You have to be prepared for rejection, or even more frustrating, no response at all. This isn't unusual. People are busy, and even if well-intentioned, they may not have time to talk to someone they don't know. Don't take this personally, and maintain your positive attitude.

Your opening words need to be your "hook," the reason someone should pay attention to you. By referring to a mutual connection such as a shared school, contact, or experience, you're improving the odds of the person speaking to you. You should mention this shared connection in the subject line of your email, your voicemail, or however you first interact with your contact. They need to know right away why it would be interesting for them to meet you. The deeper the shared experience, the better. There is always a strong chance that an alumnus or alumna from your high school or college will be willing to take a call. Sometimes an even more tenuous connection can help you reach a desired contact.

Over time, I've gotten several calls from graduates of my alma mater, and I'm always happy to talk to young alumni and provide career advice. One evening I was in my office working late after my assistant had left. My phone rang, and I answered to hear the quivering voice of a young man who said, "Hello, I am Ian Jones and I understand you also grew up in Passaic, New Jersey. I have been working as a tech specialist for a New York bank and would love to get your advice on how to become a financial analyst." Ian's cold call worked, and referring to our common hometown was a good way to get my attention.

Build Your Pipeline

Create a list of the people you would like to meet. Organize your list into categories, such as:

- → **Friendly contacts**: people you know and can reach
- → **High value contacts**: people you can reach and who would be very valuable
- → **Aspirational contacts**: people you don't know and could be very important
- → **Unknown value contacts**: people to whom you have been referred and don't know

As you consider your outreach, make sure you start the process with the easy contacts. You don't want your most important meeting to come first. You need practice, and that is why your goal is 100 people. The first ten to twenty should be low-risk conversations. They should be with people whom you know and who know you. These are people who want to help you and with whom you are likely to have pleasant and easy conversations.

Only after you have had several meetings should you add higher risk and potentially higher value meetings. You will be ready for them after some practice, and will reach another level of expertise in meeting people.

✧ Young Woman Profiled on Humans of New York[18]

I graduated last May with an accounting degree and moved to the city. But after four months I still didn't have a job. I'd probably sent out my resume to thirty different places. I couldn't afford to keep waiting for people to call me back. So I went to the strip with all the car dealerships and started going door-to-door to see if they had any openings in accounting. I've always loved cars and used to read Consumer Reports with my dad. I thought it would be a good fit. The lady at BMW was standoffish. Then I went to Audi, where they were super welcoming. But they didn't have any positions. Then I got to Jaguar/Land Rover, which was my first choice. They sat me down for an interview right away. I was there all afternoon, and then they said, 'We like what we see, can you start tomorrow?' I ran outside to call my parents. My dad was so proud of me. I was so proud of myself.

---

18. *Humans of New York*, March 2, 2016. Reprinted with permission.

Create Your Database

By identifying whom you want to talk to, you're creating a **pipeline of contacts**. You should be organized and consistent. Keep an Excel spreadsheet of the people you're hoping to reach, and update it with additional information as you meet people and stay in touch with them. Steve, the student body president from the Midwest suggests the following: "Keep a list. It sounds trivial, but make a spreadsheet of everyone you meet: who they are, what they do, when and how you met, additional comments, and when you last communicated with them. Update this list. Revisit it regularly. It is the roadmap of your network."

Here are sample column headings for your Excel file. The more information you add, the better you'll be able to appropriately follow up in the future.

1. Name of Contact
2. Email Address
3. Phone Number
4. Title
5. Company
6. Person Who Referred You
7. Date You Contacted Them
8. Type of Contact (Informational, Interview, Other Resource)
9. Meeting Date
10. Next Steps
11. Names of People They Suggested for You to Meet
12. Follow-up Potential (High, Medium, Low)
13. Something Memorable About Your Contact (birthday, interests, kids)
14. Comments

✧ Dylan, College Senior

A detailed database with 14-column headings may seem like overkill, but it's not. It's remarkably helpful, and it's a tangible product that you can refer to if you ever feel like your progress is getting you nowhere (or if your parents ask, 'How is networking going?').

Creating this database of contacts is essential in helping you manage the process of meeting people and will be valuable for you in the future. You need to be systematic and careful about whom you're targeting, when you spoke, and what action points you have agreed upon. After you start meeting people, it will be hard to remember some of the important details that will allow you to mine your network. Everyone thinks they can remember information after a meeting, but very few people can do it without organizational tools and discipline.

The more work you put into building your database of contacts, the more accurate and up-to-date the information will be. To build a valuable network that will produce ongoing results for you in the future, **you need this tracking system.** After each day of meetings, make sure you build your database and capture this important information. Do it right away.

Review your database regularly to see who can provide you with additional contacts.

Even after you've landed your job and continue to build your career, your database of contacts will be essential. The most successful people are meticulous about their database of contacts because they recognize what an asset it is. Highly successful people have hundreds of contacts, and they mine their network regularly for professional and personal benefit. Talent or sports agents, search executives, investors, and politicians have thousands of contacts. Their network is their fortune, and they guard it zealously.

A List of Helpful People

I met Julie, a successful consultant, at a conference where we were fellow panelists. Julie revealed that one key to her success was her "list of helpful people." These were not people who worked for Julie, and they were not obligated to do things for her. These people worked in other departments and supported many teams within the firm. But Julie got special attention and quicker responses because she had good relationships with them. When her IT expert had a group party, she always attended, even if people from other departments did not. When the HR specialist was fundraising for a 10k, Julie contributed. When the digital expert invited her to join the marketing team for drinks, Julie accepted.

Be Aware

Be nice to "non-helpful people" too. Your reputation comes from both types of people and how they talk about you to others.

Julie wanted to do these things not because she was going to get something in return. She was sincere in her interest in other people and made a point of maintaining relationships with her "list of helpful people." They were more than happy to help Julie when she needed it because they liked her. Julie was known at her company for getting things done, and she did so with the help of many others. Julie created an advantage for herself, one earned with sincere effort and care. People liked her and would do things for her, even if it was not their job.

You'll need a "helpful people list." In fact, you probably already have such a list in your head. Write it down. It is best to be explicit and thoughtful about your list, as it is the foundation for your "Meet 100 People" list. While it may seem like you're just creating a spreadsheet, you're really creating the edge that will separate you from the crowd.

Remember...

∞ To get started, **tell people you're looking to meet people**, and ask them for introductions.

∞ **Always take the meeting**. You never know what will result.

∞ **Create a database of contacts** and update it regularly.

Chapter Five

Prepare to Win

Give me six hours to chop down a tree and I'll spend the first four sharpening the axe.
Abraham Lincoln, the 16th President of the United States

The groundwork for a space launch is nothing short of mind-boggling. Every single detail is planned, simulated, and double-checked because the logistics are so complex and the mission is so critical. The actual space launch looks relatively easy until you think of the intense effort behind it. Even with something that looks simple, such as baking a cake, the ingredients must be purchased, measured, and mixed using the proper methods; and the cake must be baked at the right temperature and handled in the correct manner for a delicious and attractive outcome. Becoming adept at meeting people requires the same thoughtful planning.

Once you have a warm introduction, or even if you're reaching out cold, you'll need to be ready to make the "ask" and then meet that person. What do you say, and how do you say it? What are the best techniques for creating "that special connection?" How do you best prepare to succeed?

First, Know Your Audience

It's all about careful preparation. If you want to leave an impression and boost your chances of success, you need to know as much as possible about the person you're meeting. The easiest source is online. Just Google them. Study their LinkedIn profile or any other online presence such as a blog or their bio.

By learning about their interests, you have a better chance of creating a bond. Your goal is to find the mutual interest or shared experiences that will make the person want to spend time with you and help you. Even if it is a warm referral, the person you're meeting may have other connections to you. Maybe they went to your high school or love Asian cuisine as much as you do.

Do Your Homework

You should also research your contact's company and the important people leading it. You should know the name of the CEO or head of any organization you interview with. Study the company's website to understand their products and services, and read any press releases, recent announcements, or biographies. Review their mission statement to get a grasp of their values and culture. Get a sense of the company's competition and investigate one or two of their competitors. The more knowledgeable you are, the more you'll have to talk about, and the smarter you'll seem. You'll make an instant positive impression by saying, "I recently read about the new product your company launched," or, "I saw that you recently spoke at the Northwest Healthcare Conference."

I love the story I heard of a business executive who wanted to make a big impression on a potential client. In addition to hours of work on the actual presentation, the executive learned that the client's mother grew up in Cincinnati, Ohio and was of Hungarian descent. He located the well-known Hungarian bakery in the client's hometown, purchased their famous flaky cherry strudel, and served them at the client's presentation. The executive went to that level of detail to show he cared, and "went the extra mile" to make it personal. He won the contract.

✧–*Nora, Culinary Student*

In my first semester of culinary school, I learned that one of the most prestigious and unique bakeries in the city had a job opening. This bakery used little-known, old-world methods of making bread by hand using locally-sourced wheat. I spent many hours on the bakery's website, learning all I could about their political and social mission and their sustainable methods of production. I had no experience in a bakeshop and hadn't yet completed a single pastry course, but I arrived at the interview armed with a strong understanding of the bakery's ethos and a list of meaningful questions. Despite my lack of experience, I was hired on the spot for one of the most coveted jobs in the city.

Camille is a college student and a good friend of my daughter since high school. I'd met her many times over the years. One day my daughter asked if Camille could meet me for coffee to discuss careers in marketing and, of course, I said yes. I would do anything for my three children and their friends, as most parents would. Camille was a "strong tie."

When I met her at the appointed time, I was immediately impressed. I could see how seriously Camille took our informational meeting. She came dressed as if for an interview and had a notebook with a long list of questions. Her demeanor and preparation showed that she was already ahead of the game in the art of networking. I gave her some suggestions and advice which I know made her more knowledgeable in her "real" interviews later on. Needless to say, she easily landed a summer internship.

When getting ready for your meeting, be focused and thorough, but don't go overboard. When I suggest you write a list of questions, I mean a short list of one to two pages, not twenty pages. Do not go into an interview and read from your prepared list. Let the conversation flow naturally, and know when to ask your questions in an authentic way.

An informational meeting is one where you are seeking to learn more about a career or industry. Your goal is to gather knowledge and make a connection to your contact so they will want to help you. This is clearly different from an actual job interview where you are seeking a particular role. In either case, you should go in well-prepared.

6 STEPS TO PREP

1. Do your research on the industry, company, and the individual.
2. Get up-to-date on current events.
3. List ten thoughtful questions you wish to ask.
4. Anticipate questions you might be asked, and produce short responses.
5. Write down three or four brief stories that illustrate your strengths and accomplishments.
6. Practice interviewing by doing several mock interviews with friends or family.

10 QUESTIONS TO IMPRESS

1. How did you get started in your career?
2. Who influenced you the most in your career?
3. What has been the most satisfying aspect of your job?
4. How did your career evolve from when you first began?
5. What were some of the surprises along the way?
6. If you were starting fresh today, what career would you pursue, and why?
7. What changes and trends are you seeing in your industry?
8. Do you have suggestions for courses I should take, or other ways to prepare to pursue a career in your industry?
9. What have been the greatest challenges you've overcome?
10. Would you share some of the most important lessons you've learned along the way?

Taylor, Continued

Managing nervousness is the biggest challenge in the beginning, and I found that the best way to feel more comfortable was to be as prepared as possible. I wrote my list of questions, did several mock interviews, and researched each person I met. I know my preparation was ultimately the key to my success. I found out on LinkedIn that one of the last people who'd interviewed me was directly linked to Jason, the person I'd worked for the prior summer. I called Jason right away and told him about my interview with Dan, his connection. I asked Jason if he would provide a reference for me, and he said yes. I know that referral really mattered, and I wouldn't have known about Jason's connection to Dan without the research I'd done.

Manage Your Media

Social media is both a great resource for finding information about others and also an excellent way for you to build your brand and allow others to find you. Technology allows us to be connected in ways that are almost boundless. We can easily communicate with almost anyone, anywhere in the world. We can also dig up more information about others than ever before. As of January 2017, LinkedIn has over 467 million members.[19] Facebook has over 1.79 billion users.[20] Both social platforms are ever-expanding global networks. Influencers of every sort establish their brand using social networks.

You should be thinking of yourself as a brand, too. How do you want to be perceived? How do your friends, followers, affiliations, and activities reflect on you? How should you be adjusting your social media presence to build your brand and expand your network? You're establishing the building blocks of your social media presence now. You'll enhance it over your career, but lay a solid foundation today. Curating your online persona is critical, and young people need to take this seriously early on. Employers use online sources for hiring and referencing. Take time to review your social media presence. Is it the most flattering picture of you?

Handle with Care

19. LinkedIn website as of 1/19/2017.

20. As of third quarter 2016, Facebook.

Is there anything you don't want in the public eye? If not, delete it. Look at your social presence as an employer. **Would you hire you?**

✧Grace, Senior Human Resources Executive

There is so much information that can be accessed by employers and recruiters on social media. What you say, post, follow, and like can influence your prospects of employment. If you haven't checked the privacy settings for your social media accounts, do it now. Better yet, remove anything you think is embarrassing or might not reflect the professional brand you wish to build. If you wouldn't show it to your family, you can bet your employer shouldn't see it.

Imagine yourself ten years from now looking at your photos, tweets, blogs, and videos. Do you think you'll be embarrassed or ashamed, or will you still be proud of what you've said and done? It's up to you. **Make the choice that feels right for you, not just today, but for who you want to be tomorrow.** Remember that in certain states, even arrests for misdemeanors are posted online for anyone to find. This could be a big problem. You can control this by making good choices, and it isn't something you only need to worry about when first starting out. There are too many examples of people who do foolish things that later in life they deeply regret. If you don't want to read about it in the *Wall Street Journal* or your local newspaper, don't do it.

Be Aware

If you'd be embarrassed for an employer to discover something about you, **do not do it, do not post it, and do not share it.** It isn't worth jeopardizing your future for what might seem "funny" today.

I got a call one day from an anonymous college student asking for my advice. One night he and his friends played a silly prank and took a sign from a building, which he promptly returned the next morning. Unfortunately, it was too late. The sign had been reported as stolen to the police, and the young man was caught red-handed returning the sign. While the prank might seem like a minor offense, especially since he returned the sign, it became a nightmare for him. He'd gone to court over it, and his case was still under review. He asked me if he had to tell his employer about his arrest and the pending court decision. His summer internship was highly sought after, and could lead to a prized full-time job. He'd jeopardized an amazing opportunity for a foolish prank. I advised him to tell the truth. I would have far more sympathy for someone who was honest and accountable for his actions than someone who'd lied on his application or tried to conceal an important fact about his past. If you're caught hiding something, trust is lost, and the job will certainly be lost, too.

A Winning Profile

For business or job-related purposes, make sure you take the time to create a thoughtful LinkedIn profile. Look at other profiles that you admire. Study the profiles of people a few years older than you and see how they are constructed. Think creatively about the words you use to describe yourself and your accomplishments. The strategy is much the same as creating a good resume. Make your profile short, to the point, and memorable. Also remember to include key words for online search engines. This "metadata" will help others find you by searching for the skills you have to offer.

Refresh Your Connections

Having hundreds of Facebook friends does not mean you have hundreds of genuine connections. From time to time, comb through your connections and re-engage with those with whom you've lost touch. Having hundreds of LinkedIn connections can be similarly misleading. Your LinkedIn contacts should be a curated list of people you have actually met or with whom you have some deeper level of contact. You might add some people you don't know yet, especially if they are reaching out to you with a specific request. You want your LinkedIn network to be valuable so make sure there is a good reason for each connection.

Think carefully about your "elevator pitch," the two or three sentences you would use to quickly tell someone about yourself. Use this brief summary for your LinkedIn profile and as part of your outreach to others.

There are other online platforms to explore outside of Facebook and LinkedIn. Joining alumni groups or other professional industry groups adds to your social presence and certainly expands your potential network. If you have the opportunity to write or create content, take advantage of it, whether it's writing an article, posting content on social media, or maintaining a blog.

Social media makes it incredibly easy to stay in touch with people. For example, LinkedIn makes it "stupid simple." It informs you when someone from your network is celebrating an anniversary or a birthday, and actually writes the message for you. All you have to do is swipe and hit send, which takes all of two seconds. If you spend another ten seconds to add a few words to make it personal, you will make a more memorable impact. Be genuine, not generic. You're staying in touch and staying top of mind, so people remember you.

Be Smart

Everybody likes to be celebrated. Wishing someone a happy birthday is such an easy thing, and it brings real joy and recognition. I keep track of the birthdays of my family, friends, colleagues, and network. I enjoy saying happy birthday to others, and I know it makes them smile. It's an example of how social media can be leveraged to stay in touch. It's free. Why not do it?

The Eleventh Commandment

The final aspect of preparation is how to make the all-important "ask." How do you approach the people who can help you, and how do you ask for their guidance?

Be Smart

The more specific the request, the better someone can help you, or realize that they can't. In either case, you're not wasting anyone's time.

When I was going through a career transition, I took my own advice of meeting 100 people. I reached out to former colleagues, business associates, and friends. Several people gave me golden nuggets of advice. Peter, one of my favorite former colleagues, told me something I'll never forget. He said, "Pat, everyone wants to help you, but most people don't know how. **You need to help them help you**. If you're specific in what you ask for, they can direct their efforts and help you most effectively."

What Peter meant is that it isn't sufficient to ask for general help, such as, "I need a job," or, "I want to meet more people." The effective strategy is to say, "I would like to meet Brad Button, head of recruiting, someone I know you know," or, "I am interested in working at EY, do you have any contacts there?" In time you will have a better idea of what help you need. Don't be afraid to ask for it.

"The 11th commandment: if you don't ask, you don't get."
Mario Gabelli, noted American investor and fund manager

Reaching Out

Think carefully about the best way to reach out to someone for the first time. Email is usually the easiest initial outreach. It is non-intrusive and can be read whenever it's convenient for the recipient. I don't recommend sending an email first thing on Monday morning unless you promised to send one then. Monday morning is generally a busy time for any professional, so the email is likely to get lost in the shuffle. Monday afternoon or other days of the week are preferable. Many people are reluctant to send emails outside of normal office hours or on weekends, but in today's 24/7 culture, I believe an email sent during off hours has a better chance of standing out and getting read. By sending an email on a Saturday or Sunday, or late in the evening or early in the morning, you remove it from the daily deluge most people receive during working hours. Not everyone reads emails on weekends, but many people do, including me.

Marketers and public relations executives are the experts on when to send an email for the highest open and engagement rates. They say Tuesdays get good results. At my former company, we always sent our monthly newsletter on Tuesdays, either before or after lunch, to get higher than average open rates.

Be Smart

When reaching out by email, pay special attention to the subject line. Subject lines such as "Hello," "Reaching out," or, "Would you meet with me?" are not eye-catching. You will certainly get overlooked or dismissed as spam. Again, be specific in your approach with subject lines, such as "Derrick Gray referred me to you," "Saw your quote in The Mercury News," or "Would love to discuss trends in robotics." Give them a reason to open your email.

Included in the appendix on pages 174-176 are samples of two types of outreach emails. The first are emails asking for a warm referral, although if you can ask in person or over the phone, that works well too. The "ask" will be the same.

The second set of emails are for requesting an informational meeting based upon a warm referral. These samples can be easily modified to be more direct and based upon a mutual interest if there isn't a warm referral, and if the email is a "cold" outreach.

Remember that when reaching out to someone, whether it's a person who can provide you with a warm referral or someone you want to meet with directly, you should make sure the request is short, to the point, and engaging in some small way. It must be polite, easy to read, and simple to understand.

When you request a meeting or a phone call, suggest dates and times, but be flexible. You're asking for the favor, so you need to conform to someone else's schedule. Busy people generally have trouble carving out an hour to meet someone for an informational session, or even an interview. Thirty minutes is more common. However, you need to be accommodating so that if they do want to spend more time with you, you are available. While you're asking only for ten to fifteen minutes, carve out one hour. Do not schedule yourself back-to-back with other meetings.

When you ask for only ten to fifteen minutes of someone's time, they are likely to give you that, and maybe more.

Unless you know there is a specific job opportunity, requesting an informational meeting works well. It reduces the pressure on your contact and increases the likelihood they will talk to you. Sometimes they can help you, and many times they will, but it is best not to create that expectation upfront.

The "ask" should be to get an in-person meeting if at all possible. In-person meetings are truly the best ways to create a connection for the simple reason that the person gets to meet you and see you. It is far easier to remember someone you've met versus someone you spoke to on the phone or have emailed with. Your goal is the in-person, face-to-face meeting. But sometimes you may need a phone call to get things started, and if so, you must do a good job speaking on the phone. Ideally, if a phone conversation goes well, you'll ask for a follow-up at a later date so you can meet face-to-face. The meeting is the objective, because that is how you build real connections.

That Extra Push

Sending an email or making a phone call doesn't mean you'll get an immediate response. Some people are very busy, traveling, or away on vacation. If you get no response within a week, it is perfectly acceptable to follow up on the email you sent the week before. It is fine to email and say you recognize the individual is very busy, but that you wanted to check back in and see if a short meeting is possible on a certain date. It is you who must be proactive, and it is up to you to follow up. You cannot expect an immediate response, and do not get annoyed if you haven't heard back. If you still don't receive a response after your second outreach, then perhaps this person cannot help you. No worries. Just move on to the next person on your list, and keep persisting.

In your introductory email, indicate that you will place a call to follow-up on the email. Then when you speak to your contact's assistant, you can say they are expecting your call, which allows you to more readily reach your contact.

I've been involved with a wonderful non-profit organization, Reach the World, for several years. Reach the World connects college students traveling abroad with classrooms in the U.S. to help create global awareness. One of my goals as chairman was to recruit a well-known person as the honoree for our annual benefit. I tapped my network to see if anyone had a connection to him. A millennial friend asked her Facebook friends if anyone knew him. Yes! Her friend was willing to forward my email to him. He responded that he could not join us on the appointed date. I offered to change the date just so he could be our honoree, but that didn't work. I realized

When you are networking or selling a product or service, sometimes a "no" is just a "maybe," and sometimes a "maybe" can turn into a "yes."

the only chance I had was to meet him in person. I discovered an event I knew he'd be attending and finally got to meet him face-to-face. I made my plea sincerely and politely. He asked me to send him the information on the event again. Finally, he said yes—another testament to the value of persistence and meeting people in person.

Now that you've prepared thoroughly, reached out to your contacts, and scheduled a meeting, you're ready for show time.

Remember...

∞ Basic preparation goes a long way. **Find out as much as you can about the person you're meeting** and their industry.

∞ **Use social media** for research and for establishing your presence.

∞ **Be specific in your requests** so that someone can easily determine if they can help you.

∞ **If you don't ask, you don't get.**

Chapter Six

⁜

It's Show Time

When you meet people, show real appreciation, then genuine curiosity.
Martha Beck, American sociologist, life coach, best-selling author and speaker

You got the meeting—congratulations! Once the initial excitement fades, you need to consider how to make the most of your time with your new contact. What is essential meeting etiquette? How do you establish a genuine connection so that your meeting becomes the start of a professional relationship that is mutually valuable? And what is the **single most important question you must ask every person you meet?**

It's Show Time

The dress rehearsals are over, and now it's show time. These meetings are your opportunity to show your stuff and focus on learning and connecting. The title of this book is ***Meet** 100 People*, and your goal should be to have **100 in-person, face-to-face, eyeball-to-eyeball meetings**. If there's distance involved, a video conference through Skype, for example, is acceptable and far superior to a phone call or email exchange. But an in-person meeting offers the best opportunity to establish a connection, to have the person care about you and truly try to help you, and to remember you long after you leave the meeting.

Henry is an outgoing guy, a real extrovert. He has more than 2,000 Facebook friends and is the life of the party. Yet even he has learned that an in-person meeting takes a business relationship to another level.

✧–Henry, College Sophomore

I like meeting people, but it's so easy to communicate by email that it feels like a real 'connection.' Although I had emailed my contact Jamie several times to get advice about jobs at his firm, I hadn't met him in person. I thought that if I really wanted him to remember me and care enough to help me, maybe I should visit him. I asked Jamie if I could drop by for ten minutes just to say hello, and he agreed. It made such a difference because now we each have a face, a real person, to associate with our interactions. I found out that Jamie was a football fan like me, and that we both loved the Giants. Now my email exchanges are more personal and enjoyable for both of us. We had to meet each other to establish this closer connection.

When and Where?

A meeting can take place anywhere: in a person's office, at Starbucks, or outside in a "walk and talk." Wherever you meet must be convenient for the person you're meeting. You have to go where they suggest. The same is true for timing. Since you're asking for the meeting, it's you who must be flexible and meet whenever your contact is available. If they propose breakfast at 7 a.m. or drinks at 5 p.m., so be it.

As you progress in your career, you can begin to suggest venues and times. And it's perfectly appropriate to meet for breakfast, coffee, lunch, drinks, or dinner. In fact, one of my favorite books is *Never Eat Alone* by Keith Ferrazzi. The title says it all. Everyone has to eat, so why not invite someone to join you? This advice applies both to your career and your entire life. Invite a colleague, friend, or someone you want to meet with for lunch, coffee, or drinks. Never eat (or drink) alone!

Remember the Basics

The logistics and execution of a meeting may seem obvious, but these basic elements are frequently forgotten in the frenzy of nerves preceding a meeting. Make sure:

→ You're well rested and energetic. How you feel matters.
→ You have taken care of bodily needs, such as eating and using the restroom.
→ Your clothing and shoes are clean, neat, and appropriate.
→ Your personal grooming is in order: hair, nails, and cleanliness. Avoid overwhelming assaults on the senses, such as strong fragrances. Nothing about you should be a distraction from the conversation itself.
→ You know where you're going and have ample time to get there.

Be Aware

Start out earlier than you think you need to, because you must account for traffic delays, getting lost, parking, red lights, or lines at the reception desk. You have to add ten to fifteen minutes at minimum onto what you think you need. If someone says your meeting is at 3:00 pm, be there at 2:45 pm.

Techniques to Increase Your Confidence

Before the meeting, motivate yourself with a positive attitude and do all that you can to feel confident. According to Amy Cuddy, a professor at Harvard Business School and an expert on body language, power posing (standing straight and tall) and stretching your body right before a meeting will increase your confidence.[21] Your posture matters. **Stand and sit straight and tall.** Notice how your posture influences how you feel and how others perceive you. Your clothes matter, too. If you're well-dressed, you'll feel more confident.

Anticipate the meeting with excitement rather than fear. Trust that you'll learn.

Make sure you're completely prepared and have followed the suggestions in the previous chapter. Good preparation leads to good outcomes. Go in with a good attitude and a growth mindset that's focused on engaging and learning. If you approach each meeting with genuine interest, the experience will be rewarding. It's more difficult to be nervous when you're well-prepared and excited about meeting someone new.

✧ Henry, Continued

You have to have the attitude of 'I want to be here, I'm benefitting from this, I'm lucky to be here, and I need to take advantage of this opportunity.' If you're scared #$%*less or annoyed that you have to be there, it will be obvious and the meeting will be useless.

The Meeting Starts Before the Meeting Starts

When you arrive, you'll probably interact with others prior to meeting your contact, such as a receptionist, an assistant, a

21. It is well worth watching the TedTalk given by Amy Cuddy at the following link. It is one of the most viewed TedTalks: https://www.ted.com/talks/amy_cuddy_your_body_language_shapes who you are?language=en

person from human resources, or someone else who may be working for your contact.

✧ Michael, Young Professional

I received a callback for a potential job and had to fly to Chicago for the on-site interview. The company told me they'd send a van to pick me up from the airport to make my travels more convenient. The flight had been turbulent, and the van wasn't where it was supposed to be. I was nervous, in a bad mood, and just wanted to get on with the interview. I know I was brusque and unfriendly to the van driver. The same driver took me back to the airport at the end of the day. He asked about my day, and because I was tired, I did not handle myself well. Only later did I find out that the driver was part of the recruiting team, and the van ride was part of the interview. I really blew it. Lesson learned: you need to be 'on' the whole time. You can't let travel hassles or tiredness affect how you treat people. Always treat everyone with respect.

The Power of Politeness

You really don't know who has influence and who doesn't. Humans are emotional beings, and how we interact with one another creates lasting memories. People remember positive interactions, and they never forget negative ones. Tables can turn, and a person who was not in a position of power suddenly becomes influential and holds the cards. Life's path is a long one, and you never know when and in what capacity you'll meet someone again. It's wise to treat everyone well, not only because it's the right thing to do, but also because it fosters good connections.

Be Aware

How you treat everyone matters. Be polite and be engaging. You're creating an impression even before you're in the actual meeting.

Several years ago I was in a hurry to get ready for an important cocktail event, which was the next step in being admitted to a club I wanted to join for my children. I was at the dry cleaner, rushing to pick up an item, when another woman entered and politely asked, "Would you mind if I go ahead of you? I have only one item and I am in a terrible hurry." I was caught off guard. I was in a hurry, too, but I smiled and said, "Of course, please go ahead." The woman thanked me profusely, quickly paid for her item, and left. That evening, the same woman I met at the dry cleaner was one of the key individuals on the admissions committee. I was so glad I cheerfully let her go ahead of me. She remembered me, too. If I had been rude or unwilling to be helpful, I would have been deeply embarrassed.

Another example of the power of politeness is when I visited a firm in which my former company had invested. At the reception desk in the lobby of a large New York City building, I indicated whom I was visiting and which firm I was from. The receptionist smiled broadly when she heard the name of my firm and remembered Bill, our CEO, from their brief interactions. She said, "Oh, that's Bill's firm. He is the nicest, most polite man. Tell him I say hello when you see him."

Bill was a frequent visitor and clearly made a positive impression. People remember how you treat them. Let them mention you in the most positive way. Be nice to everyone. As my mother always said, **"It doesn't cost you anything to be nice, so be nice every time."**

First Impressions Matter

A good first impression is crucial, and it starts with being on time. The only way you're guaranteed to be on time is to be early. It's better to be at your destination and wait than have anyone wait for you. You have control over this. By being on time, you're showing respect, consideration, and gratitude. If you're late, you're showing the opposite. You don't want your contact wondering where you are and why you're late. If you're early, wait in the parking lot, walk around the block or sit at reception, but get to your meeting on time.

Besides being punctual, the way you say hello, your handshake, and the first words you speak create an immediate impression. Look the person in the eyes when saying hello. Shake their hand firmly, but not with a death grip. It isn't a wrestling match. If you're the nervous type, wipe your hands before the interview so your handshake is dry. Your contact doesn't want to feel like they're handling a slimy fish. Say something nice to start, such as, "Thank you so much for taking the time to meet with me." And smile. Even if you're scared and shaking inside, smile. Be happy you're there and be grateful for the opportunity.

Suggestions for appropriate opening greetings:

→ "I am really excited to meet you. I have heard so much about you from [your referral]."

→ "I have always admired your company, and I am thrilled to spend time with you and learn more."

→ "I am very interested in pursuing a career in your industry. I really appreciate your taking time to tell me about your career."

Most people you meet will want you to be comfortable and relaxed. Remember, they agreed to meet you, so they want to help you. They'll want to learn a little about you and your interests, and then you'll have the opportunity to ask questions and learn about them. Over time, you'll learn to guide the conversation to topics that you want to discuss. But at first you must allow your contact to ask you the questions, and you must listen carefully as they speak.

Listening is What Makes You Memorable

Listening is an underrated and often underutilized skill. It's ironic that some of the best conversationalists are people who listen well, rather than those who talk a lot. I've heard it said that listening is what makes you memorable. Think about that for a minute. Listening is what makes you memorable. Why is that so? Listening takes effort, focus, and maturity. It makes the other person feel respected and valued. It allows the other person to be "heard."

Being interested is even more valuable than being interesting.

An excellent book on this topic is Dr. Mark Goulston's *Just Listen*. Dr. Goulston underscores the importance of listening skills with poignant stories from both young people and senior leaders. Many people only listen with half an ear. They're already thinking of what they'll say next, rather than focusing on what is being said. Your ability to listen with intention will directly impact how well you can continue the conversation.

Listening is a critical element in meeting people and in all of life's interactions. While the meeting is about you, to some degree it is also about the other person.

When you ask questions about your contact's career or for their advice:

→ Pay close attention
→ Really focus
→ Look into their eyes
→ Sit forward in your chair
→ Be attentive
→ Smile to show you are happy to be there

The mark of a good conversationalist isn't that you can talk a lot. The mark is that you can get others to talk a lot. Thus, good schmoozers are good listeners, not good talkers.

Guy Kawasaki, Author, marketing specialist and venture capitalist

✧Aiden, Young Professional

When I started meeting people, I felt that I had to control the conversation. I thought I needed to prove I was smart, and therefore made the mistake of talking too much. By observing others, and with time and experience, I learned that it was much wiser to hold back a bit rather than offering my opinion too quickly. I realized how much I would benefit by really listening to what was being said. With deeper listening, I was able to ask more thoughtful questions and engage in better conversations.

You must be totally engaged and present in the moment to make the most of the discussion and to ensure that your body language reflects your enthusiasm. Your conversation can take many turns. It can focus on your education, your work experience, or your interests. Remember your "mosaic pieces," the stories that best convey your strengths and personal traits. These stories will help you create a connection with your contact.

Your goal is to get your contact to relate to and empathize with what you're saying. You'll develop an idea of what interests them by the questions they ask. Focus on mutual interests.

Tone and Timing

You should also be aware of your tone of voice and the timing of your speech. Your tone should reflect confidence, but not arrogance. It should be well-modulated and even. Your energy level is reflected in your tone. If you feel tired, your tone will be flat; if you're too excited, you may sound loud or shrill. Reflect on your tone when you speak to others in various situations. Similarly, be mindful of timing. Listen carefully to what your contact says, and do not interrupt him or her. Consider whether it is appropriate to add information or ask a question. Remember, you're in the meeting to listen and learn. It is more important to be humble than to show off. People are more willing to help those who are unassuming. Don't ramble, and be aware of the time allocated for the meeting.

It will take practice, but you'll learn the subtle cues and body language that indicate whether your contact is interested in what you're discussing, in which case you should continue, or if they are ready to switch topics or conclude the conversation.

Wrapping it Up

The ending of a meeting is as important as the beginning because, it allows you to do two very important things: show your gratitude for their time, and ask for what you need. Saying thank you shows respect and appreciation. If someone gave you $200, you would certainly thank them. The individual's time is worth money, and in many ways, more precious than cash. The time they give to you can never be recaptured.

Be Smart

If the meeting was informational but you're looking for a job, say so. Tell them you would love to work in the industry or for that company. Make sure your contact knows you're interested in pursuing any opportunities that might arise.

Hopefully you gathered a lot of information during your meeting, and it's important to acknowledge it. If the meeting was an interview, it's essential for you to indicate your interest in the job (assuming you are interested). People respond to enthusiasm and energy. If you want to work for the company, say so with conviction. Tell them what you can do for them, why you would be a great addition to the team, and why you are the best person they can hire for the role in question.

The Single Most Important Question

The one question you **must** ask at some point in your meeting is, **“Are there two or three other people you recommend I talk to?”** Most people forget to do this, but it’s a question that will almost always expand your network.

Only with additional warm referrals and introductions can you effectively reach your goal of meeting 100 people. Each conversation should yield two or three additional people to meet. Once you have met ten people, you should have another twenty to thirty people in your pipeline. By the time you have met thirty people, you’ll have nearly reached your goal of having 100 prospects to meet.

Be Smart

Asking "Who else could you refer me to?" will result in valuable warm referrals from a good source.

The habit of asking about other contacts will benefit you throughout your career. In my experience, asking a contact for a referral is something few people do. Salespeople are notoriously negligent in asking their customers for additional potential customers, yet current customers are the best sources for new ones. Researchers rarely ask the simple question, “Who

10 People x 2-3 Referrals =
20 to 30 Prospects

30 People x 2-3 Referrals =
60 to 90 Prospects

else would you recommend we talk to?" Even when hiring new employees, companies typically don't ask their own employees who they would recommend to join the company. Such referrals are known as "low hanging fruit," meaning low cost (or effort) and high reward. Whenever you seek information, you should dig deeper by asking who else can be consulted, who else knows more, or who else can be helpful. Most people do not ask these questions, and they lose opportunities.

Meetings Won't Always Go Well

Despite all your preparation and planning, not every meeting will go well. Some will be cut short, and others will drag on too long. Some will generate great energy in both you and your contact, while others will discourage you. You need stamina, perseverance, and a positive attitude. You must take a long-term view and understand that how you feel about the meeting today may not be how you feel about the meeting several months or years in the future.

When I was in business school, I interviewed for several jobs and received my share of "dings." There is one rejection that has stuck with me for more than thirty years. I'd had a good interview and was very disappointed when my prospective employer, Jim, called to say that I wouldn't move on to the next round. But he did this in the most polite way possible. I felt good, despite the bad news.

Coincidentally, just one year later when I was in my new job in private equity, Jim presented an opportunity to me and my colleagues. That time, I was on the client side of the table. Jim did work for us, and I got to know him better. Years later, Jim purchased the property next to my house and became my neighbor. Since then, Jim has relocated to Florida but we have stayed in touch. I have spoken to Jim about his job search, offered advice to his son on a business deal, and invested in a company Jim introduced me to. We share an interest in cycling and fitness and have become friends. The road is a long one indeed, and you can't always see past the horizon and the many interactions to follow.

Kim, a fellow panelist at a conference I attended, told the story of how she handled a challenging interview at the start of her career.

✧Kim, Experienced Professional

When I was first starting out, I had an interview with a major investment bank. The interviewer started by saying, 'I see you're a math major and you're interested in finance. What else have you got for me?' He sat back with arms crossed and stared at me. I thought to myself, 'If I have learned nothing else at college, I have learned to ask questions.' So for the next thirty minutes, I barraged him with questions. What could have been an awkward interview turned into an animated discussion. I won him over because I was not intimidated. I politely went on the offensive. We had an excellent conversation, and it was more like me interviewing him. I proceeded to the next round of interviews and ultimately got the job.

Kim rose to the challenge set by her interviewer. She took charge of the meeting, and by asking thoughtful questions, showed her mettle. You, too, can take charge.

Other meetings get off to a rough start and are grueling throughout.

✧Justin, Young Professional

One of the worst interviews I've ever had ultimately ended up being one of the most helpful. When I was a junior in college, I was introduced to Paul, a friend of my parents who had built a very successful career in the industry I was interested in. Paul was in town for business, and we met for coffee in the lobby of the hotel where he was staying. In my mind, I was hoping Paul would hire me, so I was very excited as I walked in, resume in hand. We sat down at the table, I handed Paul my resume, and the first thing he said was, 'That's your major GPA?' I had struggled in college, and I blurted out an excuse, but Paul wasn't listening. For ten minutes, I sat there as he picked apart my resume. Then, when he was done, he gave me excellent advice. Paul wasn't going to hire me, but he said that didn't mean I wasn't going to get hired in the industry if I learned to do two things. The first lesson was to own my mistakes. I had bad grades, and most of the people I was competing against had perfect grades. This didn't automatically disqualify me as long as I was honest and open when asked about it. No excuses. The second thing I needed to learn was how to guide an interview. Everyone has strengths and weaknesses, and it is essential to emphasize and focus on your strengths so people don't focus on your weaknesses. I had excellent internship experience and stellar references, and in future interviews I would walk interviewers through my resume and tell stories about my internships. Paul didn't hire me, but with the lessons I learned, someone else in the industry did.

Justin kept in touch with Paul after the meeting, and Paul responded positively. He took a special interest in Justin because Paul saw his younger self in him. Paul was tough on Justin because he cared. Three years later, Paul and Justin continue to stay in touch. The meeting Justin had with Paul wasn't really a bad meeting, although it seemed like one at the time. There will be some meetings that are much worse. Let's look at three types of bad meetings and suggestions for coping with them.

You don't learn from someone who only compliments you and reinforces what you already know. You only learn when someone challenges you, even if it is painful.

Three Types of Really Bad Meetings

The first is the no-meeting. This is when you have made an appointment, you're prepared, and for some reason, the meeting never happens. The person is too busy, they had to travel out of town at the last minute, or they made you wait for one hour just to cancel. The no-meeting can take many forms, and none of them are pleasant. So how do you deal with one?

Sometimes, a no-meeting means the person just didn't want to meet with you. You'll easily be able to tell if that's the case. If someone reneges on an agreed meeting and doesn't profusely apologize and try to make it right, you know this may be a meeting that just won't happen. Put it behind you. Develop thick skin.

However, a no-meeting could turn into a fantastic meeting at another time. If the person who cancelled wants to reschedule, give it another go. They may have had a genuine work or personal emergency. A decent person who has to cancel on you will try to make it up to you, so give them the chance. But if they cancel again, move on.

The second type of bad meeting is the **stress-test meeting**. These meetings are tough to stomach. They usually start out badly from the beginning. The person you're meeting might be rude, brusque, sharp, or challenging. They might ask you very direct questions, put you on the spot, and work hard to make you uncomfortable. They may be doing this for one of two reasons: they had a really bad day, or they are testing you to see your reaction under stress.

✧Marie, Young Professional

I was thrilled when I was invited to interview with a world-renowned publishing company—that is, until I met my interviewer. I was ushered into a small, brightly-lit room where a pop-quiz proofreading test was gruffly pushed my way before the interviewer slammed the door behind her. By the time I completed the test I'd broken a sweat, and when she returned, she offered no pleasantries or smiles. When I politely asked how she was, she didn't answer. She interrogated me for an hour with palpable antagonism. I decided the only thing to do was combat her bad attitude with positivity and refuse to stop smiling. Despite my optimism in the hot seat, I left the interview feeling like I'd been run over by a train. In the end, I got the job, not because I gave all the right answers, but because I didn't wilt under pressure.

The way a person handles another person says more about him or her than it does about you. People might not know how to deal with their own problems under stress. You have to put these meetings behind you and learn as much as you can from them. Such difficult meetings might be your most informative sessions. They'll certainly tell you a lot about you, and that is valuable. Next time, you won't be stumped at the odd or unexpected question or sweat profusely under intense interrogation. Next time you'll do better. The stress-test meeting served a purpose. It made you tougher.

A third type of bad meeting is the awkward meeting. There are some unusual people in this world. They may have personal quirks or unusual styles. Some people have very low self-esteem, and some have little self-awareness. They stonewall, overshare, talk too much, talk too little, or digress to irrelevant topics. They have personal quirks and act differently than most people.

One of my most memorable meetings was an awkward meeting. I agreed to have lunch with a woman who was recommended by someone I didn't know very well. The woman was new in town and looking for a job. As soon as we met, I was skeptical. She was uncomfortable in her own skin, overshared intimate life details, and had no clear idea of what she wanted to do. It only got more painful as the lunch went on, although I tried to put her at ease. I knew I would remember this awkward meeting because I felt empathy for someone still learning to network effectively.

You will have a really bad meeting, and it's likely you'll have more than one. These meetings can take many forms, and if you're ready, you'll survive them. In fact, really bad meetings are sometimes the most memorable of all. You'll tell your friends about them and chuckle—once you get over them.

Reflection 6: What Did You Learn?

After each meeting, take five to ten minutes to think about what you learned and what you need to do next. This debrief is useful for any work meetings you have. Add an update to your database and include something memorable about the meeting, whether it was a topic you discussed or something you noticed about the person you met. If you learned names of family members, note that. If you found out the person just came back from a vacation to Cuba, write that down. These will be memory triggers as well as reference points for the future.

Think about what you learned from the meeting, whether it was factual information or general advice. While it takes a little extra time, you won't regret having invested this effort. Relying on your memory will not be enough six months later when you want to get back in touch. If you do this right away, you will develop a valuable habit and build a rich database for yourself.

Now that you're armed with a strategy for a successful meeting, let's focus on creating that special connection.

Remember...

∞ **The meeting starts as soon as you arrive** at your destination, and only **ends once you have left** the premises.

∞ **First impressions matter.** Focus on getting the basics right.

∞ **Listen well** and you'll be remembered.

∞ Endings matter as much as beginnings. **Depart graciously**, with gratitude.

∞ **Always ask** who else you might meet.

Part 3

Cultivate

Chapter Seven

⁜

Discover Something Special

Go out, talk to people, listen to people, and
most importantly, be prepared to be amazed.
Celeste Headlee, Talk Show Host

Your number one goal in any meeting is to establish a connection, a reason for your contact to invest time and energy into helping you. How do you discover that "special something" that creates a meaningful connection? How do you nurture that connection into a stronger relationship? What mistakes should you avoid making?

Find the Treasure

Every person is unique and knows something you don't. The combination of another person's life experiences, personal characteristics, and knowledge are special. Just like you, they are a mosaic. It may take some work to find these hidden treasures within someone else, but that is the perspective with which you should go out and meet people. Finding the "bond," that common interest or natural chemistry that captures the attention and imagination of both you and your contact, is how you'll create a connection and build a relationship. There's one secret that I know works well: you need to be genuinely open and eager to learn something from everyone you meet. You need to have a curious mind.

The Basic Truths of What People Want

Several years ago at my 20th reunion at Harvard Business School, I remember hearing the results of a survey asking graduates which courses they found to be most valuable to their careers. Graduates five years out said that their finance or marketing courses were the most useful. In contrast, graduates who were twenty-five years into their careers cited courses on organizational behavior and human capital as the most useful. In fact, these experienced graduates indicated that their understanding of human psychology was critical to their leadership.

In order to build strong relationships, it is essential to understand what motivates people. Everyone wants to be heard, respected, and understood. Everyone wants to contribute, and they want their contributions to be valued. Everyone has something to offer from their own journey through life. Most people are ready to share their wisdom and hard-learned lessons. When you meet people, give them that opportunity, and listen to their stories.

Most people feel affection for their family, friends and circle of contacts. This is why warm referrals work so well. People are willing to do favors for people they care about. They're willing to spend time and effort to meet someone who's been recommended to them. They are also willing to risk their reputation, or "social currency," to arrange a meeting for someone else. People are almost always willing to help people they like. Adults are especially willing to help sons and daughters of their friends. You'll always feel greatly indebted to anyone who helps your family, friend, or colleague, and you'll want to reciprocate any way you can. This is human nature.

In addition, most everyone values their health. If you can be helpful to someone as it relates to their health, or the health of their family and friends, you're creating an important bond and a great debt of gratitude. Doctor referrals and quick access to experts are greatly valued. If someone mentions a personal health issue, or one of a family member, it is appropriate to say, "I hope you are doing better." Empathy goes a long way in building relationships. People will go out of their way to help friends in need, and they'll find ways to repay that kindness in so many ways.

Remember the things people care about the most: their family, their kids, their health, and their own success. If you can help another person with any of these, they'll always remember it, so look for opportunities to be helpful.

People feel an affinity with people similar to them in some way, such as growing up in the same area, going to the same school, or having similar interests or personalities. The search to find this similarity, or "link," is your challenge. There is an art to finding the link quickly so you can dive in, bond, and really enjoy the conversation you're having.

Similarly, people care about their careers and their personal advancement. Helping others with contacts, referrals, or relevant news or information is also a great way to build rapport. Perspectives on industry trends, opinions on products and services, ideas about how technology impacts our lives, all these topics can be applicable to someone's work. The more people you meet, the more you will develop valuable viewpoints.

An in-person meeting is the most effective way to impress someone with your curiosity, interest, appreciation, and understanding. Mutual interests and shared experiences create connections. They allow people who might otherwise seem very different to come together and learn from one another. Meeting in person allows you to listen and be heard in a personal way.

When I think of my network, which ranges from millennials to seniors and includes people of many ethnicities and backgrounds, the most common elements are personal characteristics such as high energy, enthusiasm, curiosity, and a passion for life. I have found that my passion and energy draw out similar qualities in others. Finding shared interests help create bonds, and the more research you do ahead of time, the better the chance you have that you'll find things in common.

Remember that age, gender, ethnicity and race are all irrelevant to finding the "link." The link transcends the superficial.

Your Space Reflects Your Interests

If your meeting is in someone's office or home, you have an extra advantage in finding the "link." Personal space, whether home or office, reveals what a person cares about. After all, they placed the clues. Each personal item is there because it's important in some way, whether the item is a photograph, a painting, a book, or a trophy. If you can make a polite comment about it, such as, "I love your wrestling trophy, I am a wrestler since high school," or, "I loved the book *Tribal Leadership*, I found relevance to my personal life as well as business," you're starting the process of making a connection. You must do this carefully in order to do it appropriately. The comment should be general, benign, and sincere. But in many cases, starting a conversation around an item you might see, or offering a polite compliment, can start the conversation in a positive way.

✧Kira, High School Senior

When I was meeting with a college admissions officer, one of the first things I noticed in his office was a photograph of a family skiing and the words 'Steamboat.' I immediately said, 'What a great photo! I love to ski, and my family often skis at Steamboat.' I learned that the admissions officer was an avid skier and we reminisced about our experiences. We moved on to a variety of other topics, but I know that our first 'link,' skiing, made a difference in getting us off to a great start.

Kira was a qualified candidate, but there is no question that the interview and her ability to connect with the admissions officer contributed to her acceptance at her top choice school.

Listening Well, Part Two

After observing, **listen well**. Remember, everyone wants to be heard, and most of the time they are not, because so few people can listen carefully and thoughtfully. Listening is one of the most underrated skills, yet it has the greatest payoff. **Careful listening is how you find treasures and create connections.**

Pay close attention to the questions your contact asks you. What are they most interested in on your resume? What are they seeking in you? What do they want to talk about? Listening well and showing interest will go a long way toward forging a good connection. You have to be comfortable going with the flow and allowing the exchange to evolve naturally. You might find the shared interest right at the beginning of the meeting. Sometimes the "link" surfaces in the middle of the conversation, and often you find the connection just as you're wrapping up. Don't worry about digressing and spending time talking about the mutual interest. It is okay to stray to a topic that you're both excited about, whether it's sports, current events, or your alma mater. As long as you feel like the conversation is positive and there is mutual interest, spend some time sharing and bonding. This bond will allow you to build on your relationship later.

If They Like You, They'll Help You

Whether on the phone or in person, once you have set up a time to speak to your contact, your main objective is to **get the person to like you**. It is human nature to help someone you like. Conversely, it is rare to help someone you don't like. So how do you get someone to like you?

As discussed in Chapter 2, you have to like yourself, because self-confidence is appealing. Think of your strengths. Write down the things you like about yourself. Think about the things you like in other people. People who are fun, energetic, confident, enthusiastic, and curious are generally well-liked. These traits are like magnets. Think of how you can project these positive qualities.

Everyone likes a happy person. Approach every meeting with confidence and a cheerful attitude. A smile is your best accessory. Even if your contact is having a bad day, your upbeat attitude can make a difference. Go into each meeting with the view that the person is happy to see you and excited to help you. With a positive attitude, you'll get off to a great start.

✧ Evan, College Senior

When I was a college senior at the University of Wisconsin, I met with an entrepreneur, Drew, for a potential full-time job in D.C. Drew started the meeting by asking me about my college experience. I soon learned that Drew had a son who was a high school junior and in the process of looking at colleges. I immediately offered to speak to Drew's son about the college application process and share my experience at the University of Wisconsin, a college high on his son's list. The rest of the interview went very well. I followed up by meeting Drew's son and have kept in touch with him. I met with Drew several times, too, and ended up getting the job.

Evan had a terrific opportunity to create a connection and show his willingness to be helpful to Drew's son. Opportunities like these abound. Look for them and always follow through on offers you make.

People respond well when you ask for genuine advice. Your contact wouldn't have agreed to meet you if they didn't want to be helpful. They are expecting you to ask thoughtful questions. By doing so, you're engaging them and creating a closer connection. When someone helps you, they become an ally. They want you to succeed. Do not be afraid to ask for guidance, and be open to their suggestions.

Margaret is a young woman I met two years ago when she was pursuing her MBA. She reached out to me citing several common contacts and an interest in learning more about my job. When we met, she was engaging, bright, and energetic, and I enjoyed our time together. Her enthusiasm was infectious. When she asked me to help her with a class project that related to my work, I readily agreed. I made introductions that I know were invaluable to her research. She later shared the results of her findings with me which I appreciated.

Since our first meeting, we have had lunch and coffee several times. I like Margaret, welcome her outreach, and am pleased to be able to offer advice. She has been helpful to me, too. She has made several introductions to people in her network, entrepreneurs running high-growth businesses that may become investment opportunities for me. And our relationship continues to grow. I introduced Margaret to my daughter while both were in San Francisco, and recently the three of us had dinner in New York. Margaret initiated a professional relationship, which we have turned into a friendship, one that is valuable for us both.

In fact, I have many friends whom I met along the course of my career. One friend, Harry, is particularly dear to me. I have known him for more than thirty years. He was the CEO of a company in which my firm invested, and I worked as a young associate on the team. I lost touch with Harry for several years after the company was sold, but always remembered our business relationship fondly. When my daughter attended school near the town where Harry and his wife live, I emailed him to say hello. We reconnected and bonded over Harry's love of bicycling. He invited me to join him for his annual "bike your age in miles" party. I was not a strong cycler, but his invitation motivated me to train. It was his 75th birthday, and I had never ridden longer than thirty miles. That event has become an annual outing, and our friendship has continued to grow. A few years ago, at the age of 77, Harry became an author and published the book *Fitness Beyond Fifty*. When I mentioned I was writing *Meet 100 People*, Harry was one of my most avid supporters and faithful editors. I would never have guessed when I was first starting out how important my business relationships would become later in life. He offered the following perspective on networking.

✧ Harry, Retired Executive

A dozen years ago, my son Michael, age 36, and I, age 66, went on a trip together. We started at his home in San Francisco, drove to Bend, Oregon, spent a few days there and then drove back via Crater Lake, Oregon. It was a terrific opportunity to bond. A number of times Michael mentioned things I'd done that had a significant impact on his development. I didn't recall a single one of them. I reminded him of interactions we'd had that I thought were significant. He didn't remember even one of them. I think of this when I think of networking. You never know what will stick and turn out to be important. That's why every contact has to count. Frequently the contacts you make that seem the least important at the time will turn out to be the most important.

It takes practice and effort to feel a sense of ease in meeting people. You'll likely experience false starts and pitfalls. You'll be much better at meeting person number sixty-one than person eleven. But with time, you'll refine your messages, become comfortable asking thoughtful questions, and learn to listen better. You'll find the topics that resonate with your contact and learn how to follow-up to enhance your professional relationships.

12 Ways to Create a Genuine Connection and Get Someone to Like You

1. **Be authentic and sincere.** Don't pretend to be someone you're not. You can't establish a connection with someone when you're not true to yourself.

2. **Be positive and uplifting.** Your smile is the least expensive and most beautiful accessory you have. A positive attitude will show on your face, in your body language, and with your words.

3. **Be polite and respectful.** Treat everyone with great courtesy. There is NO downside to being kind and nice.

4. **Exhibit good body language and polite habits.** Look people in the eye, sit and stand straight and tall, and lean forward to show genuine interest.

Be Smart

If you are meeting for coffee, lunch or drinks, who pays the tab? You should always offer to pay. Your contact is doing you a favor, so you should be prepared to treat them. If your contact refuses and wants to pay, then accept graciously and make sure to thank them.

5. Dress appropriately. Research the appropriate dress for your meeting. Dress can vary by region, season, and company. Err on the side of conservative. It's hard to go wrong with neutral colors and simple attire. In the startup and technology worlds, it is best not to be overdressed. The right clothing will make you feel confident.

6. Show genuine interest in your contact's words. This has to be both sincere and visible. You must look at the person directly and pay attention, which requires interest and focus. You must be present in the moment.

7. Tell a short story about you that is relevant to the conversation. People remember anecdotes far better than facts.

8. Prepare for your meeting and ask thoughtful questions. Listen well to the answers.

9. Offer a compliment or note something you genuinely like about the person. Again, a compliment doesn't cost anything, and gives a generous gift to someone else.

10. Ask for advice sincerely, and listen attentively.

11. Be helpful. Look for ways to share your experience, expertise, or connections. Remember what people care most about: family, health and their own success. Show that you can add value to them.

12. Say 'yes' whenever you can if someone offers you additional opportunities or suggestions, and especially other people you can meet. Make sure you follow through and follow up. Do it right away so you create the most positive impression.

12 Obvious Things You Must Never Do

1. Be late for your call or meeting. If you're running late, call, text or email, and say so. Politeness counts. Apologies matter.

2. Interrupt or be rude. Don't be so eager to say your piece.

3. Be negative, aggressive, or obnoxious. No one wants to help a jerk, much less work with them.

4. Talk too much or for too long. Don't tell a long, drawn-out story. Don't focus on trivial details. The details really don't matter—you do!

5. Be too quiet or too short in your responses. Talking with you shouldn't feel like pulling teeth. Don't be boring.

6. Do not exaggerate, and **never, ever** lie. You'll be found out, and your credibility will be shot.

7. Don't gossip. Telling stories, especially negative ones about others, destroys their trust in you.

8. Be uninformed. But if you don't know something, just say, "I don't know." People prefer honesty.

9. Whine, complain or blame others for your problems. Don't be immature.

10. Criticize or argue. Even if someone is combative, keep your cool. They may be testing you.

11. Make excuses, whether for your grades, lack of a job, or because of a hard life. Take ownership and be accountable.

12. Blame other people or belittle anyone. Never throw anyone under the bus. It reflects poorly on you.

Be Aware

A good sense of humor goes a long way, and there is nothing more enjoyable than someone who can make you laugh. If you have this natural gift, use it. But stay away from risky humor, as it can easily backfire and offend.

Taylor, Continued

Meeting 100 people changed the way I interact with potential employers and conduct myself in interviews. As you continue to meet people in your industry, either for formal interviews or over coffee, you realize that people respond positively to a few things. They like to see that you're prepared. Focus your effort on understanding their company. Read the news and ask a question about how a relevant current event might affect their business. Be engaged, energetic, and sincere. You want to portray confidence and make them feel like they would enjoy working with you. Finally, remember that the process is not a zero-sum game and the goal should always be to make a good impression, not simply to get hired. Not every aspect of your job search is in your control. The company's hiring needs or timing may change. The best way to maximize your chances is by leaving a good impression everywhere you go.

Review the lists above carefully. They may seem obvious, but people get these things wrong again and again. They probably make errors because they are nervous, ignorant, or rude. Do not be one of those people.

Google recently conducted a study called Project Aristotle, which involved interviewing hundreds of employees to determine what factors created the best teams. They found that the best teams consist of people who are respectful and who contribute equally. The study showed that in the long run, successful people were in fact **nice people**. Be one of *these* people.

Remember...

∞ Look and listen carefully to find a **common interest** that will link you to your contact.

∞ People help people that they like. Focus on developing **confidence, enthusiasm, energy, curiosity, and humility**.

∞ **People care about a few very basic things: their family, friends, health and career.** If you can help someone with any of these basic things, they'll be indebted to you and help you, too.

∞ **When you discover the link, spend time on it**, and note it afterward. This will be your way to stay in touch and develop the relationship.

Chapter Eight

⁜

That Personal Touch: Following Up

Gratitude is the most exquisite form of courtesy.
Jacques Maritain, French philosopher

You met someone new, made a connection and left feeling good about your meeting. Once you get home and update your database, what's next? How do you follow up in a way that maintains the connection and helps you stay "top of mind?" Many people falter on this very important step in the networking process. But you won't. Here's how you continue the conversation.

Keep the Conversation Going

After each of your meetings, it's essential to **follow up**. The follow-up can be a call, email, or a handwritten note. You're never intruding or bothering someone by saying thank you. It is a simple act of good manners. The follow-up note continues the conversation, allows you to show your gratitude, and leaves a positive impression. If you've followed up with someone and a job opportunity becomes available at their company, they're more likely to remember you and invite you for an interview. Similarly, they might refer you to a friend or colleague who's looking to hire. No matter what, follow up after every meeting with gratitude and grace.

Following up isn't just important for building your network. It's also critical in the work you do, no matter what it is. If you're a doctor, following up with patients builds a trusting relationship. If you're a salesperson, following up is essential to sealing your deals and keeping your clients happy. Follow-up truly matters and distinguishes the good from the great. Develop this habit now because it will serve you well throughout your entire career.

The most important message to convey in your follow-up is gratitude for the person's time. You must do this. Even if the meeting was short, and even if the meeting wasn't what you expected, you must say thank you in every case.

Call, Email or Handwrite a Note

You can call and say thank you, or you can send a thank-you email. You can follow up the call or email with a handwritten note and really stand out. Whichever method you choose, don't delay—do it right away, certainly within 24 hours. The sooner you do this, the better. Immediate follow-up shows respect, organization, and the ability to get things done right away. The call, email, or note doesn't have to be long. In fact, it should be short and to the point, but it should focus on reinforcing the connection you are creating.

The following is a template for a simple thank-you email, which you can customize for your own use.

Dear Warren,

Thank you so much for taking the time to meet with me Friday morning. Your insight about preparing for a career in marketing was incredibly helpful. Hearing about your career reinforced my strong desire to work in the consumer products industry. I hope one day I have as successful a career as you do.

I'm continuing to pursue digital marketing roles in Atlanta and will reach out to John Locke as you suggested. Please let me know if there is anyone else you suggest I speak to. I have attached my updated resume. Here's hoping the Hoyas win the basketball game next week.

Best regards and thank you again,

Jay

The email is simple, straightforward, and short. Yet it still conveys Jay's continued interest in digital marketing, reminds Joe of their mutual interest in Georgetown basketball (the Hoyas), and very importantly, repeats the request for additional connections.

✧Hallie, Young Professional

Just letting someone know that you appreciate the time they took to talk to you shows gratitude and thoughtfulness, and it reminds them you're still there. If you think you'll ask them for advice or a favor in the future, checking in with them occasionally really helps. Even if you don't think the relationship will go any further, it's still important to follow up, because you can't predict what either of you might need in the future. And always respond to people when they reach out to you. Life gets busy, but it only takes five minutes to respond to an email or phone call, and you never know where it could lead.

The Personal Touch

Very few people take the time to hand write a note, and this gesture will be appreciated and remembered. That is the objective: to be remembered. You can even write a brief email saying thank you, followed by a longer handwritten note.

Dear Pat,

I cannot thank you enough for our wonderful meeting this morning. You were so wise and helpful about everything career-related and you have such an amazing story to tell. Thank you for sharing it. I would love to get the contact information for the marketing professionals you mentioned at the two firms so I can reach out to them per your suggestion.

Your insight was invaluable, and I truly appreciate the time you took from your busy schedule to meet me. You're now number one on my list of 100 to meet! I hope to see you around campus next weekend!

Leigh

Think of how you would feel after getting such a polite and thoughtful note. You can be sure I'm happy to continue helping Leigh. I do not expect to receive notes like these, but it's wonderful when I do get them.

Below is a letter I received from a young man, the son of a long-time friend of mine, to whom I provided some career advice over the phone. I hadn't seen the young man in many years, but lasting friendships matter, and I was happy to provide advice and give him my "meet 100 people" pitch.

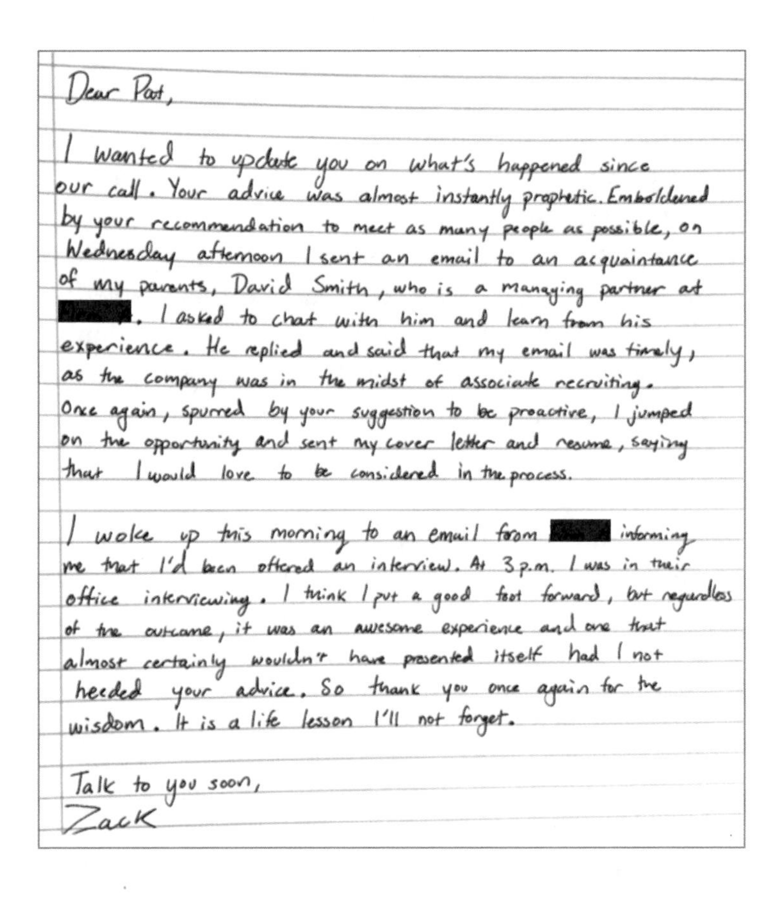

Dear Pat,

I wanted to update you on what's happened since our call. Your advice was almost instantly prophetic. Emboldened by your recommendation to meet as many people as possible, on Wednesday afternoon I sent an email to an acquaintance of my parents, David Smith, who is a managing partner at █████. I asked to chat with him and learn from his experience. He replied and said that my email was timely, as the company was in the midst of associate recruiting. Once again, spurred by your suggestion to be proactive, I jumped on the opportunity and sent my cover letter and resume, saying that I would love to be considered in the process.

I woke up this morning to an email from █████ informing me that I'd been offered an interview. At 3 p.m. I was in their office interviewing. I think I put a good foot forward, but regardless of the outcome, it was an awesome experience and one that almost certainly wouldn't have presented itself had I not heeded your advice. So thank you once again for the wisdom. It is a life lesson I'll not forget.

Talk to you soon,
Zack

Zack did a number of things well in this follow-up letter. First, he showed sincere gratitude for the time I spent with him. He was engaging and complimentary, and his note made me feel appreciated. Second, he gave me an example of what he did and how it worked out for him. Zack showed me that he truly listened during our conversation, understood what we discussed, and put it into action. Regardless of whether Zack got the job, I'm thrilled to have inspired him to be proactive and meet people. I am curious to hear more.

When you write your follow-up note, refer to the advice your contact gave you and show that you took it to heart. Leigh mentioned my advice to meet 100 people, and Zack demonstrated how he benefited from my advice. In both cases, Leigh and Zack clearly showed that they were engaged and willing to act on my suggestions.

When someone you meet offers suggestions, be sure to write them down so you can refer back to them, whether it's for a follow-up or for use in your own life. You'll undoubtedly collect nuggets of wisdom along the way. Hopefully you can pass them on to others over time.

Be Smart

When someone suggests a contact for you to meet, it is perfectly fine for you to ask one of two things: "Would you introduce me to the recommended person by email or phone?" or, "May I use your name when reaching out to that person?" **Then follow-up and make sure you pursue these new connections**, and circle back and thank the person who referred you.

Cultivate the Seed

Taylor was thrilled when he finally got his job after 108 meetings. In his excitement to start work, he assumed the "meet 100 people" process had ended. But the real value in meeting people is in the relationships you've begun to develop along the way. Taylor met 108 people, and some of those connections carried the seed of a meaningful relationship. The perfect opportunity for Taylor to get back in touch with them was to let them know he succeeded in his job search. He emailed his contacts to thank them again for their role in his success. Taylor shared his new email address and promised to call when he was in town for coffee. Most people sent congratulatory replies. It was the perfect way to stay in touch.

Taylor, Continued

So you've done it. You've met 100 people, now there's another step: maintain and curate your network. Your network is alive, and needs to be periodically nourished. If you keep your network vibrant, you can rely on it to help you as you continue to build a career. People want to be helpful, and everyone would prefer to help someone they've known for a long time. If you let your network stagnate, you'll eventually have to rebuild it all over again.

In each meeting, you will plant a seed. The seed is the memory of who you are. For a seed to grow, it needs attention: sunshine, water, and weeding. If you want your contact to become a valuable part of your network, someone you regard as a mentor, friend, or resource, you'll need to put in effort to cultivate that connection. This means staying in touch and deliberately tending to the relationship.

How do you build a relationship with someone you've just met? Make it a priority to stay in touch. Your networking database should indicate the last time you spoke, emailed, or met with your key contacts, and you must commit to an outreach on a regular basis. For some people it might be monthly, while for others a quarterly "touch base" is sufficient. In either case, you need to have a strategy for staying "top of mind." You'll have to allocate time, once a week at minimum, to review your list and reach out to those who are due for a "catch up."

When you find ways to be helpful to your contacts, you strengthen your connection with them. Reach out in a way that makes it easy for them to re-engage, such as asking a question or offering an invitation to which they can respond. With each interaction, your relationship will grow.

Be Smart

If you don't stay "top of mind," someone or something else will take your place. It's up to you to make the outreach. Find a way to stay on the radar so opportunities continue to find you.

Suggestions for Cultivating Relationships

→ **Email the person with an article you're certain will be of interest to them, either about their company, their industry, or other topics they enjoy.**

Sample Email

Dear Jared,

I'm attaching an article about major technology trends in the automotive industry. Since we talked about how tech companies were disrupting transportation when we met several months ago, I thought of you when I read this and thought you would enjoy it too.

I would love to know your reaction. Let me know when we can catch up.

→ **Email your key contacts list as soon as something special happens to you. The most obvious and easiest time to send an update is when you get a new job.**

Sample Email

Dear Joe,

I'm emailing to thank you again for meeting with me in June. I still remember our conversation and how much you inspired me to pursue a career in family law. I'm thrilled to let you know that I received a job offer from my first-choice firm and will be starting next week. It is a happy conclusion to my job search, and you were an important part of that process. Looking forward to keeping in touch.

→ Call or email the person when you know of a conference or an event they might be interested in and that you might be attending, too. Invite them to join you if it's appropriate.

Sample Email

Dear Jane,

I am planning on attending the Writer's Digest Conference in two weeks and I wanted to see if you might be there, too. If you are, I would enjoy seeing you again and finding out how things are going for you. I would love to get coffee and update you on my recent work. I still chuckle when I think of the great time we had at lunch in November.

Looking forward to hearing from you.

→ Call or email if there is a social or athletic event that the person might have an interest in, or that you might invite them to.

Sample Email

Dear James,

I remember our conversation several months ago about our mutual interest in bike racing. I'll be riding in the upcoming Tri-State Bike Challenge and wanted to see if you're planning to go. It should be a fantastic day for biking, and it would be great to see you again. Let me know if you're attending and we can coordinate when we might meet. Here's hoping for sunny skies and cool temperatures.

→ See if your contact might want to join you for a non-profit event.

Sample Email

Dear Rebecca,

As I mentioned, I'm involved with a non-profit organization called Reach the World. Since you expressed interest in learning more about Reach the World, I wondered if you might join me at their annual benefit in March. It is sure to be fun, as I will have several other young entrepreneurs there, and the honoree is a well-known celebrity. I would be so thrilled if you could join me at my table.

I am looking forward to seeing you again soon.

→ Reach out to your contact when you have met a mutual friend.

Sample Email

Dear Roger,

I bumped into Joe the other day and it reminded me of the last dinner we all had together at The Best Steakhouse. I hadn't heard from you in a while and thought I would check in and say hello. Hope all is well. Let me know if you might be free for coffee or lunch in the next couple of weeks. It would be great to see you. Let me know what works for you.

Please give my regards to Sara. Talk to you soon.

Reaching out to the contacts in your network on a regular basis will make sure you stay top of mind. Even if you have had a lapse in communication, there are always valid reasons like the ones suggested above to reach out again. New job opportunities, resources, and other connections come out of this regular contact. It is up to you to make the outreach. You have to be proactive and send a note, call, or email to keep the connection strong. **Nurture your network.** Build it and develop it by helping others. The benefits last a lifetime.

✧Ann, Professional Re-entering the Workforce

The idea of finding a job after a long hiatus was intimidating, but I had a network that I could re-activate to start the process. I was amazed by how quickly a few phone calls and meetings led to employment. My best advice for anyone is to maintain your contacts, as they are a lifeline to opportunities. Even if you haven't been in touch for a while, it's okay to reach out and re-connect.

You and Your Network

Your ability to do your job, help your contacts, and build your career will be directly influenced by this continuous nurturing of your network. Just like meeting 100 people, keeping in touch with them will have a similar payoff. The ability to cultivate relationships will increase the value of your network and make your professional and personal life more successful. Any job involving interaction with clients will require you to stay in touch so you can benefit from new sales, projects, and job openings. Just like friendships need to be nurtured in order to remain meaningful and relevant, professional contacts need similar attention. Identify those who are important to you, stay in touch, and add value to their lives.

Andrew, Young Professional

I had been in my job for four years and was trying to relocate to New York. I'd stayed in touch with several of the people I met in my first job search, and when I mentioned I was looking for opportunities, I quickly had several introductions and referrals in New York. My second job search was significantly easier because of the relationships I'd built over the last four years.

Reflection 7: Review and Reach Out

Make time at least once a month to review your database of contacts and see whom you should reach out to. Develop a plan for the month, listing whom you plan to email, call, or meet again. Never eat alone—use mealtimes to build relationships. Create a list of what you plan to do each week, and cross off each item once you have completed it. Make it a regular practice to reflect and review your connections and your outreach plans.

Remember...

∞ To get maximum value from your meeting, you must **follow-up right away.**

∞ **Call, email, or hand write a note** thanking your contact for their time.

∞ The follow-up is the best way to continue the dialogue you've just had. **Refer to what you shared in your conversation, ask for additional advice, and keep them engaged**.

∞ **Your follow-up makes you memorable** and distinguishes you from the rest.

Chapter Nine

⁜

Never Stop Growing

The keeper of your career will be not your employer but your personal network—so you'd better put a lot of effort into making it as extensive and as vital as possible.

Nicholas Lemann, "The Network Man,"
The New Yorker, *October 12, 2015*

You proactively met 100 people to build your network, and now you have a job that will propel your career. Congratulate yourself on your excellent work, but remember that from your very first day on the job, the process of meeting others is far from over. In many ways, it is just beginning.

Why should you keep meeting people after you've landed the job or even after you're well into your career? What's the best way to keep in contact with your first 100 people, and how are the techniques for networking within an organization different from those you used before? How do you become so fluent in meeting people that it's a habit you'll practice all your life? Think back to the "lucky" few who think they have it all figured out. You may be one of the smart and aggressive people who got his or her first job right out of college and didn't have to do much interviewing. You

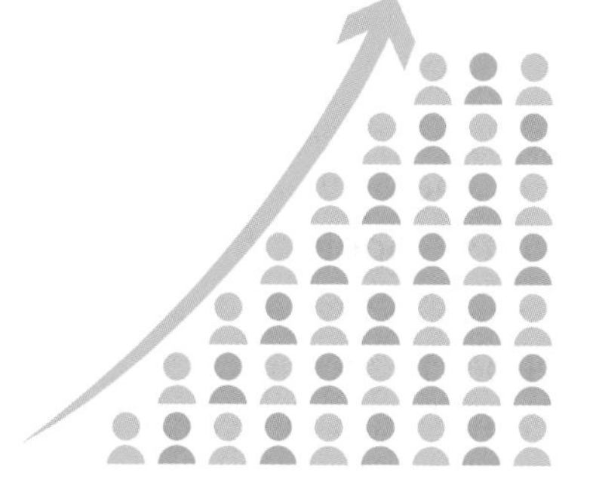

have a fantastic job without having to meet 100 people! You think you're ahead of your peers and will be the quickest up the ladder. Think again, because you missed a priceless opportunity to begin building your network during a time when people are most ready and willing to meet you.

✧Natalie, College Student

I was one of the lucky ones. I studied computer science, and as a female, I was in high demand. I got a summer internship junior year and received an offer of full-time employment right away. Most people would have just taken the job offer and breezed through their senior year with one major worry behind them. My perspective was different. I told my potential employer that I was thrilled about the offer, but requested a month to continue meeting people and interviewing. The employer agreed and took the chance that I might work for someone else. I went on to meet more people and survived many grueling interviews. I got to see how other firms conducted their business, and I gained better awareness of my market value. I received four additional job offers, and while some of them were tempting, I ultimately accepted the original offer. The role was competitive in its compensation, but more importantly, I really liked the people, and their flexibility impressed me. I am now employed there full-time and recruit new hires. Since I'd interviewed with many firms, I became a better recruiter. My firm has actually benefitted from allowing me to have had additional interviews.

The very best time to start or expand your network is when you're looking for a job, because you have a clear reason for asking others to meet with you and offer their advice. Sometimes the job process is so stressful that as soon as you land your dream job, you're ready to sign the offer letter and be done with the process. While Taylor's experience was drawn out in meeting 108 people, in the end he gained a huge advantage over the person who interviewed with one firm and got the offer right away. Taylor has a broad network and has honed skills he couldn't have learned any other way than by meeting more than 100 people.

Is it worth the investment to continue interviewing once you have a job offer? It depends on you. Perhaps you should break off the process with other firms who haven't yet given you an offer. It also might be worth extending your response time to the firm who's given the offer. You certainly don't want to jeopardize the offer in hand, but Natalie's experience is telling. She only asked for a short time before responding to her company. She met just a handful of other firms, not another 100 people. Meeting more people was valuable because she extended her network, gained a better understanding of other firms in the industry, and got a better sense of her own capabilities. It's highly likely that within the next five years, she will be looking for other opportunities. Her early experience with interviewing and the connections she made will undoubtedly help her.

Never Stop Networking

Networking has to remain a priority for continued success even after you've landed a job. You should focus on meeting people within your company, your industry peers, and colleagues who are more experienced than you are.

In his book *Alliance*, Reid Hoffman provides an insightful look at the alliance between employees and employers necessary to build loyalty and trust. With no assurance of long-term employment for anyone now, Hoffman suggests having honest conversations about goals and objectives, and emphasizes the need for rotational opportunities or "tours of duty" to give people great experiences and exposure to others so that companies get the most of their talented workforce. Knowing this, the importance of meeting 100 people only increases. You need to develop your own set of allies within your firm.

Many people forget that some of their most valuable contacts are their colleagues and the warm referrals they can provide. These relationships are not only important for your career progression (promotions are often influenced by a broader group or committee), but these networks will contribute to your own level of expertise. Get to know not just the people in your own department, but those in other departments. Aim to meet 100 people in your firm and the ecosystem around it. The best time to start this process is right at the beginning. People are usually very willing to talk to the new person.

Internal networking is making sure you know the people within your firm. Networking with your own colleagues is easy—have lunch, go out to drinks, and attend social events. Get to meetings a bit early, close your laptop and engage with others before a meeting starts. Go to the cafeteria and meet someone new. All of these activities build relationships that make work more enjoyable and nourish your network.

Make it a point to spend quality time with your superiors and get to know them as people, not just colleagues. If you get the opportunity for business travel, spend meaningful time with your work colleagues. Take the same train or flight so you can get to know each other better. Turn off your digital device and have a conversation. Have meals with them or explore a new city together during your downtime.

Downtime during business travel is one of the best times for connecting with new people. If you are offered an upgrade when traveling, take it. Go to the business class lounge and talk to your seatmate. If you get the opportunity to attend an event or conference that might be a bit expensive, consider saying "yes" and making the investment. As a young business executive once said to me, "Putting yourself in the same room with people at a higher pay grade is a fast way to get there yourself."

Be Smart

Find ways to make sure you are out and about in places where influential people gather. If you don't have much money, put aside a few dollars per month for your networking fund. Take someone to lunch or dinner. Dip into this fund for that event, course, or other opportunity that you otherwise might not be able to afford.

Plan Your Next Step

You must have a specific plan with objectives and benchmarks in order to keep meeting 100 people once you have a job. Continue building your original database with contacts from your "list of helpful people." Again, review your database regularly and make sure to reach out to people you haven't communicated with in a while. Don't let six months pass with no communication, and don't wait for them to reach out to you. Take charge and reach out. Whenever new opportunities present themselves, take them. I love Sheryl Sandberg's book *Lean In*, and find its advice to be relevant for people regardless of gender, age, or background. Sandberg encourages everyone, especially women, to "lean in" and say yes when offered new roles, whether you feel fully qualified or not. Say "yes" and see how things work out. Trust yourself and believe you can learn. You do not need to have all the expertise for any role or project right away. What you do need is the ability to learn and find those who can teach you. You need to keep meeting people to accomplish this.

In addition, always be ready to go to meetings. Part of this is being dressed for the part. If you work in a professional setting and business attire is appropriate, be prepared. Have a jacket (and for men, a tie) handy, and always look professional. Ask to join meetings when appropriate. Be proactive. You have nothing to lose by asking to join a meeting, because if you don't ask, you may not be invited anyway. Asking to attend a meeting shows interest, ambition, and desire. When you have the chance to meet people outside your company at industry events such as conferences, go. These are ideal settings for meeting people inside your industry but outside of your organization. Through interacting with them, you'll learn how others approach jobs similar to yours and what's trending in your industry. Find out what competitors are saying about your company and how others perceive it. You'll get much better information than you would by reading newspapers, magazines, and online articles. Journalists are just people who meet a lot of people and record their views. Be like a journalist. Meet people and find out as much as you can.

"**It isn't what you know, but who you know**" is a well-known adage, yet some people don't fully understand how important it is. What you know does matter, but who you know matters more. It isn't only about the influence the other person wields. **Each person you know is a gateway to another set of skills**. Who you know becomes part of who you are. Each person's influence on you shapes your thinking, which in turn influences your actions. Connections are valuable not only for how they'll help you, but also for how they'll inspire and motivate you to reach your full potential. Your network is like a reservoir from which you can continually draw, helping both yourself and others to achieve goals. And just like a reservoir needs to be replenished so it doesn't run dry, you must revitalize your network by meeting more people and sharing your contacts with others so this ecosystem remains vibrant.

Join Peer Groups and Industry Associations

There are many ways to meet other people in your industry and cross-industries. General conferences allow you to do this. If you're in a functional role, such as HR, finance, marketing, sales, or IT, go to conferences targeted at your function. When I was promoted to a new role in which I was inexperienced, the first thing I did was find a peer group to join so I could learn from others. If a peer group doesn't exist, organize one. Invite one to two others for coffee and have them invite peers. The group will grow. People want to meet others in similar circumstances.

Some companies are much more sophisticated than others, and you want to know who does things best. With a broad perspective, you'll know what best practices are. Keep meeting people and asking questions until you become an expert. As you advance in your career, others will seek your expertise. You may be offered opportunities to speak on panels or at conferences. Say yes, even if you feel out of your comfort zone. Getting out of your comfort zone is the only way to grow.

Opportunities come your way when you speak at a conference.

I've been asked to speak at many events, and I've made a conscious decision to accept as often as possible. There were many times when doing so was inconvenient or uncomfortable. I once spoke at a conference in Jaipur, India in front of 600 people. Getting to India required a fourteen-hour flight, and when my connection to Jaipur was delayed, I felt extra pressure. I was nervous and doubted myself many times while preparing for the event. But I did it anyway. And now when I am asked to speak in front of smaller audiences, I always think: it can't be as bad as speaking in front of 600 people in Jaipur. After each speaking engagement, I am truly grateful I participated, because each time I learn something new. You will, too. I've identified senior executives I wanted to meet based on hearing them speak at conferences. This is not uncommon. High-priced executive recruiters scour conferences to identify talented people and grow their networks.

If you're focused on an industry such as financial services, healthcare, or technology, go to industry events. Know your competition. If you have the opportunity, learn from others who are in different industries too.

In addition to learning more about your own industry and meeting people in similar roles, make it a priority to meet people in different industries, too. Only then can you have a broader perspective of best practices and who is truly pioneering. I like to think of technology companies as trendsetters and ones to watch for knowledge-sharing, innovation, and employee best practices. They have to hire the best and the brightest to remain at the forefront. They are experts in identifying the most talented people and motivating them.

Learning what your peers within technology or other leading-edge companies are doing can inspire you to think of ways you can improve your organization.

In the Know

As soon as you have a job, you're the one "in the know." People will start reaching out to you for meetings and advice. Many people were generous with their time when you started the process of meeting 100 people. Now you can pay it forward.

You'll have countless opportunities to help others build their networks. Once you have a job, you'll be creating new networks, both internally and externally. You'll recruit new hires. You'll go to conferences. You'll be involved in alumni associations and various other organizations. You'll become someone whom others seek out for guidance. Eventually, you'll likely have the chance to recruit. Take advantage of it. Recruiting has a specific goal: to identify and attract the best talent to your company. The only way you'll know what good talent looks like is to meet a lot of people and develop pattern recognition to identify them quickly.

Now you'll be on the other side of the table. You get to ask the questions and determine whether the person has the skills, experiences, and personal qualities that will add value to your company. The more people you know, the better you'll be at recruiting, which will increase your worth at work. Finding great talent is a highly sought-after skill. As an investor, I have found that CEOs and investors spend a significant portion of their time thinking about talent and talent-related issues, because great talent makes for great companies.

To continue paying it forward, get involved in alumni associations and take an interest in those who are just starting out. Help them in the same way that others helped you. You can do this through alumni interviewing and mentoring programs and by encouraging your company to recruit on campus. You can host groups of students who are interested in your industry or provide informational meetings on campus. All of these opportunities provide value to others and will impart benefits to you, too. Take an interest in the younger people at work. Identify those you wish to mentor as they learn the ropes.

Networking should be a life-long commitment. You'll find that the more you give, the greater joy you'll receive from your interactions. Your network will continue to grow and become more valuable with each contact you add.

Meeting 100 people is available to anyone. Make it a priority, establish a plan, tell others about your goals, and keep going. The benefits are tremendous and achievable.

Remember...

∞ Once you have a job, **your networking is just beginning**.

∞ Meet 100 people **at work and outside of work**.

∞ **Networking is a life-long endeavor**. The more people you meet, the more valuable you become.

Taylor, In Conclusion

I now receive calls from younger professionals asking for advice, and I make time in my schedule to talk to them. I proactively develop relationships at my firm and I go out of my way to make new contacts. I keep in regular touch with a handful of contacts on my growing list of people. When I see an article that would be of particular interest to someone I've met, I send it to that person. I congratulate my contacts on successful developments when their company appears in the news. I try to reach out at least four times a year. A week into the New Year is an ideal time to reach out and say Happy New Year, with an offer to meet up in the coming weeks.

Meeting 100 people was the best 'graduate course' I could have taken to prepare me for my career. I know that my network is, and will continue to be, the lifeblood of my professional and personal success.

Chapter Ten

⁜

Pay it Forward

What you get by achieving your goals
isn't as important as what you become
by achieving your goals.

Henry David Thoreau, American essayist, poet, and philosopher

I could not have written this book ten years ago. I wouldn't have had the wisdom or the stories to provide good advice twenty years ago. It truly took me more than thirty years to see the full value in proactively and systematically making networking and meeting people a part of my life. I've been enriched in so many ways by each person I've met, both in my career and my personal life.

This book is my way of paying it forward, offering my insights and experiences to make it just a little easier for you, regardless of what stage of your career or life you're in. It's meant to give you a head start and to encourage you, especially if you don't think you're skilled at meeting people. The more people you meet, the more comfortable you'll be. The more you do anything, the better you'll get at it.

In *Outliers*, Malcolm Gladwell, another of my favorite authors, makes a compelling case for the need for many hours of practice to be good at anything. He cites 10,000 hours as a foundation for real mastery. Talking to people is no different. Those who seem especially eloquent and at ease in social and professional settings have likely put in a lot of time to get there. It is counterintuitive, but that which looks easy took a tremendous amount of hard work.

Any endeavor starts with one step, one outreach, one first meeting. Make a plan, set a goal, and start reaching out. I know the benefits are there for you.

So now go out and **meet 100 people**. They are waiting to meet you!

If you liked *Meet 100 People*, **tell your friends**.

If you would like to share your stories and experiences, **email me** at pat@meet100people.com.

For additional thoughts and suggestions, visit Meet 100 People on **Facebook** and **Twitter**.

Good luck, and stay in touch.

Pat

Recommended Reading

1. *Give and Take: A Revolutionary Approach to Success* by Adam Grant
There are three ways to engage with someone: you provide reciprocally, you take, or you give. Adam argues it is those who give without expecting a benefit that ultimately gain the most.

2. *Just Listen: Discover the Secret to Getting Through to Absolutely Anyone* by Mark Goulston
Everyone seeks to be heard, and the greatest gift one can give is truly listening to what someone else is saying. It shows respect and uncovers better ways to relate.

3. *Never Eat Alone: And Other Secrets to Success, One Relationship at a Time* by Keith Ferrazzi
Keith extols the values of networking and building meaningful relationships, offering sound advice on how networking should be part of your daily life.

4. *Mindset: The New Psychology of Success* by Carol Dweck
A life-altering book that describes how a growth mindset fundamentally sets you free to be your best.

5. *Tribal Leadership: Leveraging Natural Groups to Build a Thriving Organization* by Dave Logan
Dave provides a framework for understanding organizations and the cultures embedded within them. The perspectives are relevant for how to live, as well as how to create the right work environments.

6. *The Alliance: Managing Talent in a Networked Age* by Reid Hoffman
Reid provides thoughtful advice to employees and employers on how to find mutual benefits, both short-term and long-term, when knowing that very few people will stay with one firm for an extended time.

7. *The Defining Decade: Why Your Twenties Matter and How to Make the Most of Them* by Meg Jay
Meg provides advice on how to make the most of your twenties in order to position yourself well for the rest of your life and career.

8. *Lean In: Women, Work and the Will to Lead* by Sheryl Sandberg
While targeted at women, Sheryl challenges us all to take advantage of opportunities and give life our best effort.

9. *Quiet: The Power of Introverts in a World that Can't Stop Talking* by Susan Cain
Susan posits that one third of the population are natural introverts. She offers counsel on how this quality is a strength for those who possess it, and for those who live and work with introverts.

10. *Grit: The Power of Passion and Perseverance* by Angela Duckworth
A brilliant book describing one of the most important ingredients for success: grit. Angela relates excellent stories and inspirational anecdotes.

11. *Outliers: The Story of Success* by Malcolm Gladwell
Malcolm explores the many factors that contribute to unusual achievement and what makes successful people different from others.

12. *The Bigs* by Ben Carpenter
Ben offers an insightful view of a career in finance through his own experiences in the industry and his observations of young professionals starting their careers.

13. *Designing Your Life: How to Build a Well-Lived, Joyful Life* by Bill Burnet and Dave Evans
Professors for one of Stanford University's most popular courses, Bill and Dave apply design principles to building a meaningful life.

More Inspiration

¶ "Your visions will become clear only when you can look into your own heart. Who looks outside, dreams; who looks inside, awakes." *—C. G. Jung, Swiss psychotherapist*

¶ "It's not about the external work, it's about the internal work." *—Will Smith, actor, producer and philanthropist*

¶ "Your values become your destiny." *—Mahatma Gandhi, leader of the peaceful independence movement in India*

¶ "The human species thinks in metaphors and learns through stories." *—May Catherine Bateson, American writer and anthropologist*

¶ "The will to win means nothing without the will to prepare." *—Juma Ikangaa, 1989 NYC Marathon Winner*

¶ "By failing to prepare, you're preparing to fail." *—Benjamin Franklin, author, politician, and scientist*

¶ "Social media is an amazing tool, but it's really the face-to-face interaction that makes a long-term impact." *—Felicia Day, American actress, comedian, writer and creator of the web series, The Guild*

¶ "Giving connects two people, the giver and the receiver, and this connection gives birth to a new sense of belonging." *—Deepak Chopra, American author and public speaker*

¶ "Diligent follow-up and follow-through will set you apart from the crowd and communicate excellence." *—John C. Maxwell, American author, speaker, and pastor*

¶ "The harder you work, the luckier you get." *—Gary Player, retired South African golfer*

¶ "Ambition is the path to success. Persistence is the vehicle you drive in." *—Bill Bradley, U.S. Senator from N.J., professional basketball player*

¶ "All men should strive to learn before they die, what they are running from, and to, and why." *—James Thurber, American cartoonist, author, and journalist*

¶ "A human being becomes whole not in virtue of a relation to himself but rather in virtue of an authentic relation to another human being." *—Martin Buber, Austrian-born Israeli 20th century philosopher*

¶ "Know thyself." *—Inscription at the Delphic Oracle*

¶ "A well-designed life is a marvelous portfolio of experiences, of adventures, of failures that taught you important lessons, of hardships that made you stronger and helped you know yourself better, and of achievements and satisfactions." *—Bill Burnet and Dave Evans,* Designing Your Life: How to Build a Well-Lived, Joyful Life

Appendix A: Sample Resumes

Sample Resume I

Bobbie Best

100 Main Avenue
Clifton, NJ 07014

973-777-6654
bbest@gmail.com

EDUCATION

The Best University 2014 - 2017
Bachelor of Arts New York, NY

- Major: Marketing | Minor: Digital Media
- Coursework included Communications, Digital Media Design, Advanced Marketing Strategy
- GPA: 3.25 / 4.00 | Major GPA: 3.81 / 4.00

Clifton High School 2009 - 2014
High School Diploma Clifton, NJ

- Coursework included AP English, AP Calculus and AP Italian
- SAT: 2100 / 2400 (Math: 700, Verbal: 700, Written: 700)
- Extracurricular activities: Varsity Track, Jazz Trumpet, Future Business Professionals

PROFESSIONAL EXPERIENCE

Stunning Magazine May - August 2016
Intern New York, NY

- Cold calling advertising leads, prepared for promotional events and provided general office management organizing online files and documents
- Participated in designing magazine layouts and advertising spreads

University Journal January 2014 - Present
Marketing Team Member New York, NY

- Helped develop and execute marketing and advertising plan for this college publication
- Organized and managed several events including a launch party with 300 attendees

Marketing Weekly May - August 2015
Summer Intern Jersey City, NJ

- Created database for major prospecting campaign targeting potential advertisers in the Northeast
- Helped improve website and social media presence by revising content and adding graphics, increased Facebook followers by 250,000

Brook Haven Club June - August 2009, 2010, 2011
Senior Sailing Instructor Woodcliff Lake, NJ

- Assisted with general sailing instruction and supervision of children ages 4 to 10
- Ensured a safe, fun and educational sailing experience for young campers

SKILLS AND INTERESTS

- Proficient Italian, fluent in Spanish
- Advanced skills with Microsoft Office and a variety of social media
- Completed five half marathons and training for NY marathon
- Interests include travel, cooking and playing the trumpet

Sample Resume II

Beatrice A. Mazing

22 Brook St.
Milford, CT 06914

203-222-5113
bamazing@gmail.com

EDUCATION

University of Maryland — September 2015 - Present
Bachelor of Science in Biology — College Park, MD

- Coursework in Psychology, Biology and Advanced Mathematics
- GPA: 4.0/4.0; first year honors, selected for accelerated biology program

Silver Spring High School — September 2011 – June 2015
Diploma with honors — Silver Spring, MD

- GPA: 3.6 / 4.0; high honor roll all four years
- National Honor Society, Music Honor Society
- Varsity Lacrosse, Varsity Field Hockey, Varsity Tennis

PROFESSIONAL EXPERIENCE

UMD Emergency Response — May - August 2015
Emergency Response Crew — College Park, MD

- Work with emergency response team on 911 calls on the weekends and evenings
- Experience with over 500 transports to local hospital
- Commended for "staying cool under pressure"

Milford Medical Group — May - August 2015
Clinical Assistant Intern — Milford, CT

- Assisted with minor medical procedures
- Organized patient scheduling and pre-visit questions

Milford Community Center — May – August 2014
Head of Children's Activities — Milford, CT

- Supported head of programs, organized activities and schedules
- Supervised ten instructors managing 200 children

SKILLS AND INTERESTS

- Skills and certifications: Lifeguard, First Aid, CPR certified
- Proficient in Microsoft Office Suite, EPIC healthcare software
- Enjoys 19th century French literature
- Avid bicycler completing several charity and century rides

Sample Resume III

Ina N. Credible

7 Kensington Avenue
Austin, TX 73301

203-555-1212
incredible@gmail.com

PROFESSIONAL EXPERIENCE

Bank of the Southwest July 2014 - August 2016
Lead Client Services Representative Houston, TX

- Provided superior client services to clients in the asset management group of a major regional bank serving high net worth clients with average assets over $25 million
- Helped improve response rates by 50%, increased throughput by 25%
- Assisted in recruiting and training new client services representatives
- Promoted twice in a two year time-frame and profiled in Bank of the Southwest's new hire brochure as a rising star

Southwest Credit Union May – August 2013
Summer Intern Houston, TX

- Led a project to analyze potential customers for a new product service offering which launched successfully the following year
- Worked across groups to get feedback from various team members regarding new initiatives which ended up in 20% cost savings from the prior year
- Helped organize summer outing for all summer interns and managers

The Banking Report May - August 2012
Circulation intern Plano, TX

- Analyzed circulation base for this blog focused on trends in US regional banks
- Managed outreach to potential subscribers and increased circulation by 25,000 with a targeted social media campaign.

EDUCATION

University of the Southwest 2011 - 2014
Bachelor of Arts New York, NY

Major: History | Minor: Chinese
GPA: 3.25 / 4.00 | Major GPA: 3.81 / 4.00

Student body president in senior year. Managed a budget of over $400,000 for a campus of 10,000 students.

SKILLS AND INTERESTS

- Proficient Chinese, fluent in Spanish
- Advanced skills with Microsoft Office and a variety of social media
- Five time state chess champion
- Interests include salsa dancing, Asian cooking and poker

Appendix B: Sample Outreach Emails

SAMPLE OUTREACH #1

Dear Professor Smith,

As you know, I am very excited about pursuing a career in financial services, and Finance 101 has only increased my interest and enthusiasm. You have mentioned Joe Topman during class discussion several times as someone who often comes to recruit for students. I'll be in NY in October and would love the opportunity to reach out to him and meet him for a brief informational meeting. May I ask you to provide an introduction to him?

I am attaching my resume for your reference. Thank you so much.

John Kay

SAMPLE OUTREACH #2

Hello Karen,

I know that my dad mentioned to you that I am very interested in meeting Jane Coder when I am out in San Francisco interviewing for jobs. Since Jane is such a successful engineer, I wanted to see if you might be willing to introduce me to her so I can ask her for a brief informational meeting. I would love to learn how she got her start and how she likes living in San Francisco.

I am attaching my resume for your reference. Thank you so much, I really appreciate it. I am looking forward to seeing you at Thanksgiving.

Mary Lee Grace

SAMPLE OUTREACH #3

Dear Dr. Season,

My parents suggested I reach out to you and ask if you might be willing to provide an introduction to Dr. Raven. You have always been an inspiration to me as I have pursued my studies to become a doctor. I feel that the more people I meet in the profession, the more I'll learn about how to best prepare and ultimately become a caring healthcare practitioner. Thank you so much for all your help.

I am attaching my resume for your reference. I am looking forward to seeing you the next time I am home from college.

Mindy Earnest

SAMPLE OUTREACH #4

Dear Joe,

My economics professor Marty Smith was kind enough to suggest that I reach out to you to see if you might be willing to meet with me for an informational interview and career guidance.

I am currently a junior at Georgetown and I am very interested in becoming a financial analyst. You have had such a successful career in the financial services industry, I would love to get your advice on how I might seek internships and best prepare myself to become a financial analyst.

I'll be in NY on October 10th and could meet anytime that is convenient for you. I am attaching my resume for your reference. Thank you in advance for your time and consideration.

With gratitude,
John Kay

SAMPLE OUTREACH #5

Dear Jane,

I am a junior at MIT studying computer engineering and was referred to you by my neighbor, Karen Jones, who spoke very highly of you. I am interested in learning more about a career as a software engineer, and I wanted to see if you might be willing to meet me for coffee next week when I'll be visiting San Francisco. I would love to hear about your experience as a successful engineer in a highly competitive field. I am available anytime on March 3rd, 4th, or 5th, whatever time and location is most convenient for you.,

I am attaching my resume for your reference. Thank you so much in advance for your willingness to meet me.

With gratitude,
Mary Lee Grace

SAMPLE OUTREACH #6

Dear Dr. Raven,

Dr. Martin Season is a good friend of my parents and he suggested I reach out to you. I am applying for internships prior to applying to medical school. I would love the opportunity to meet with you, even if only for 15 minutes, to get your advice on the best way to prepare for a career as a doctor. I'll be in Boston on April 4th if that might be convenient for you.

I am attaching my resume for your reference. I really appreciate your time and am very grateful for the possible opportunity to learn more from an eminent physician like you.

With real gratitude,
Mindy Earnest

Bibliography

1. Names of individuals and certain situations have been disguised to protect privacy.

2. National Center for Education Statistics, 2013-14.

3. Svrluga, Susan, "More Than 4 out of 5 Students Graduate Without a Job. How Could Colleges Change That?" *The Washington Post*, January 30, 2015.

4. Express Employment Professionals, 2014.

5. Forrester Research, 2016.

6. According to a 2014 study by the Freelancers Union, in 2020 more than 40% of U.S. employees will be self-employed.

7. Byron Wien, Blackstone Market Commentary.
https://www.blackstone.com/media/press-releases/article/blackstone's-byron-wien-discusses-lessons-learned-in-his-first-80-years

8. Ibid.

9. Keith Kragh, Chairman and CEO of DocuSign, speaking at EY's 2016 Strategic Growth Forum.

10. I learned this useful construct from Beth Chase, founder and CEO of C3 Consulting.

11. Chamorro-Premuzic, "Why You Lack Self-Awareness and What to Do About It," *Fast Company*, March 10, 2015.

12. For a long list of strengths, see the following link.
http://examples.yourdictionary.com/examples-of-strengths.html#4lAwSlvdyihWlo24.97

13. Longer lists of values can be found at the following links.
https://www.akpsi.org/admin/document.doc?id=486
https://www.stevepavlina.com/articles/list-of-values.htm

14. See additional information about resumes at the following link.
https://www.alumni.hbs.edu/careers/navigating-your-career/making-a-career-change/Pages/resumes-and-cover-letters.aspx

15. Granovetter, Mark, "The Strength of Weak Ties," 1973.

16. Ibid.

17. Ibid.

18. *Humans of New York*, March 2, 2016. Reprinted with permission.

19. LinkedIn website as of 1/19/2017.

20. As of third quarter 2016, Facebook.

21. It is well worth watching the TedTalk given by Amy Cuddy at the following link. It is one of the most viewed TedTalks.
https://www.ted.com/talks/amy_cuddy_your_body_language_shapes who you are?language=en

Acknowledgments

A book is never a solo effort, especially one entitled *Meet 100 People*. Each one of us is a product of the people we have met and with whom we are connected. I have been tremendously fortunate to have a wonderful and broad network of colleagues, former colleagues, friends, and family.

Among my network are those who inspire and those who support just by being there. There are those who push and light the fire to get going and keep at it. And there are those who apply real expertise to help create a finished product. I have had the incredible benefit of all these amazing individuals helping me to complete *Meet 100 People*.

Thank you to my editor, Laura Himel. You are truly amazing with a work ethic and a sense of style and quality that is unparalleled. You helped make this book more concise, appealing, and artistic than I could have imagined. Thank you to Julie Vaughn, who took up the mantle of creating images and artwork which help tell the story in a memorable visual way. You helped translate my ideas into a consistent theme of appealing imagery.

I extend my gratitude to all who have read and re-read *Meet 100 People* and provided invaluable comments and suggestions. A special thank you to Harry Gaines, who showed me that writing a book at any age is possible and even fun! Lorraine Ash, your enthusiasm gave me the push I needed to get started. Thank you to Ann Woodward for sitting with me at Garelick and Herbs and saying, "You need to write this book," and then keeping after me to do it. I am grateful to Regina Pitaro whose feedback I treasure as it comes from the heart.

I greatly appreciate all the entrepreneurs I have met, especially in the last two years, in particular Nick Farina and Beth Chase, who have been incredibly helpful with ideas and suggestions. As the founders of all the companies I have invested in know, I am a huge fan. You inspire me with your energy, enthusiasm, and drive. You wouldn't have gotten to where you are without an amazing ability to connect with people. Your examples shine in my mind.

If I hadn't met Cathy Kinney, this book would not have happened. She took me under her wing and introduced me to a group of her colleagues who had lunch regularly. I was the new person, but they made me feel like one of them from the start. Through Cathy I met Lisa Carnoy, and Lisa is the source of this book's title and the reason I wrote it. I am forever grateful for your kindness and generosity. Lisa, you have inspired hundreds of people, and you will influence countless more.

You cannot spend thirty years at one company and not be fundamentally impacted by the amazing people around you. Each of my former partners at General Atlantic is a 'master networker,' and I kept learning from you each day for thirty years. I've learned countless lessons at GA. One of the most important is that life is a long game, and it is essential to do the right thing.

I have met many young people over the course of my career whose experiences, stories, and examples helped shape my thinking and understanding about what is important. I have taken those ideas and am sending them back to a wider audience so others can benefit.

The list is long and there are so many others near and dear to my heart. Heidi, Karen, and Margharet, thank you for our coffees and walks. It is our special way to maintain our connection to one another. To DG7, you know who you are. Same with my GF friends.

For the many young people who provided comments, suggestions, and inspiration, especially Andrew, Leigh, Zach, Maggie, Athena, Rebecca, Alexa, Sarah, Alana, Sophia, Chris, Kat, David, Kenny, Margaret, Meredith, and many, many others.

My deepest gratitude goes to my family: Jon, for your patience and steadfast support; William, for your inspiration and good humor; Nicole, for your deep integrity and practical good sense; and Chris, for your passion and drive. Yvette, you are a great sister and an amazing proofreader. And to my mom, who gave me the most important gifts of all: my life and my values.

About the Author

Pat Hedley is an advisor to and investor in innovative growth companies. A visionary and strategist with a broad, global network of experts and resources, Pat counsels CEOs, entrepreneurs, and management teams. Previously she was a managing director with General Atlantic, a global growth equity firm. She is Chairman of Reach the World, a non-profit organization promoting global awareness. Pat has an MBA from Harvard Business School and a degree in computer science from Dartmouth College.

Notes